**Illinois Central College
Learning Resources Center**

Improving Your Writing Skills

Improving Your Writing Skills

A Learning Plan for Adults

Jerold W. Apps

Follett Publishing Company
Chicago, Illinois

Atlanta, Georgia • Dallas, Texas
Sacramento, California • Warrensburg, Missouri

Designed by Karen A. Yops

Library of Congress Cataloging in Publication Data

Apps, Jerold W., 1934–
   Improving your writing skills.

   Includes index.
   1. English language—Rhetoric.   2. English language—
Business English.   3. Authorship.   I. Title.
PE1408.A64   808'.042   82-5130
ISBN 0-695-81668-3   AACR2

First Printing

Contents

The current crisis in communication, common myths about
writing, and what it takes to write better.

How to assess your writing problems and develop a learning plan.
How to do a weekly time inventory and lay out a systematic plan
for solving writing problems.

Where to find information, including personal experiences, libraries,
and other people. How to organize research for writing and
determine the accuracy of facts.

Preface

Walk into any bookstore, and you'll see several books on how to improve your writing. What makes this one different? First, this book is written for those adults who must write as a part of their day-to-day activities, who don't particularly enjoy writing, yet who realize the importance of good writing and want to improve.

Second, this book takes a different approach. It starts with a guide for assessing writing problems and then suggests a way of correcting them—a "learning plan." The book explains how to select courses, conferences, correspondence programs, and other resources based on the time available for study, the cost, and the writing problems to be solved. Also included are instructions on how to keep a Writing Log, a record of how various writing problems are approached that also provides an opportunity for writing in a nonpressure situation. Writing exercises are presented throughout the book so the reader can practice immediately the various skills discussed.

Improving Your Writing Skills is based on three assumptions:

1. It takes time to improve writing skills.
2. Writing skills are most easily improved by starting with the writing tasks at hand.
3. Writing skills are improved by writing and rewriting and writing and rewriting, interspersed with some analysis and study.

I owe a thanks to many for this book. First, Professor Robert E. Gard, now retired, who invited me to teach nonfiction writing at the Rhinelander School of Arts twelve years ago. Much of this book comes from the suggestions of several hundred students who attended those writing classes over the years. Many of them wanted to learn how to write better because their jobs demanded it, and they were looking for help.

A special thanks to those who read this manuscript and offered critical comments: Professor James Sparks, chairperson, Mental Health Continuing Education Programs, University of Wisconsin–Extension; Vida Stanius, Rossman Consulting Associates, Chicago; Steven Schmidt, who returned to school and is now completing a graduate degree at the University of Wisconsin–Madison; Hayward Allen, Credit Union National Organization; and Sheila Mulcahy, writer and editor, University of Wisconsin–Extension.

For continued support and encouragement, I especially want to thank my editor, A. Jean Lesher.

Also thanks to a very special team of cooperative and competent typists who helped make sure deadlines were met: Karen Wideen, Sally Gurske, Julie Gilman, Pat Sullivan, and Cheryl Seitz.

Chapter 1

Writing Happily When You'd Rather Not Write at All

Thousands of people must write, yet they really don't like to do it. Some even hate it. Nevertheless, every day they must write reports, letters, memos, or proposals; or if they are in college, they face term papers, essay examinations, theses, or dissertations. Many would prefer to do almost anything else, but to survive they must write. So they write, for better or for worse—often worse. They suffer from their shortcomings and bore their readers with vague generalities or mind-boggling details.

It's not that these people don't have the potential for improving their writing skills. Their problem is attitude, and that is what we need to deal with first.

You and Your Writing

Why are you interested in improving your writing skills? (I assume you are interested; otherwise, you wouldn't be reading this book.) Perhaps you're bored with your own writing. It lacks sparkle. You detest writing, and when you're finished, you're not at all happy with the results. Or more likely, others are not happy with the results—those who have to *read* what you write. You may wish to improve your writing skills because someone close to you—your boss, an office colleague, your spouse, or your instructor—has told you subtly, or maybe not so subtly, that your writing needs help. And after getting over your initial hurt feelings, you've decided to do something about it.

Perhaps you have recently enrolled in school to complete an undergraduate degree started many years ago, to work on a graduate degree, or to begin college or university training for the first time. You've discovered after a month or six weeks in the classroom that if you're going to survive, you must improve your writing. (I read many student papers each year. I search through many essay examinations for the answers to the questions. Most of the time, those students who have adequate writing skills come out ahead.) And if you're just now considering graduate school, you may have to demonstrate your writing ability before even being considered for admission.

Perhaps you have a new job that requires you to write more than any of your previous jobs. Or you've watched those who have been promoted in your present firm, and it's evident that those with the better writing skills have an edge at promotion time. Most firms need people who can communicate with the written word. It's a valuable asset.

Aside from such practical considerations, there is another reason to be concerned about your writing that you may be unaware of: the close connection that exists between clear thinking and clear writing. To write clearly, you must think clearly. Muddled thinking usually produces muddled writing. (Although, conversely, clear thinking doesn't always precede clear writing.) The very process of writing, particularly if you're trying to do your very best, is an aid to clear thinking. The two work hand in hand. As you write, you'll find that your ideas and their relationship to one another usually come into sharper focus.

Not only does writing help you think more clearly, but it also stimulates deeper areas of thinking, hidden meanings you never realized before. The process of writing can tap the unconscious mind to get at the root of problems, simplify what seemed complex, or uncover complexities in what seemed simple. The process of writing is one link to the unconscious. At times you may not realize what you know about a subject. When you begin writing, however, words begin to pour out, ideas come into focus, examples mysteriously appear on the page. You surprise yourself.

A certain prestige and influence come with being read and understood. Those who have developed their writing skills influence far more people with the written word than do many with the spoken word. As Byron wrote:

> But words are things; and a small drop of ink,
> Falling like dew, upon a thought produces
> That which makes thousands, perhaps millions
> Think.

There is a personal satisfaction that comes with mastering a craft, and writing is certainly a craft. The satisfaction of writing comes from being able to communicate your ideas so others will understand.

A National Communication Crisis

Many people whose business it is to communicate, simply do not communicate well. These people are in responsible positions where their writing and speaking make a difference. They are government leaders, teachers in colleges and universities, business and professional people. Yet they have great difficulty producing a sentence or a paragraph that says what they want to say. Granted, sometimes would-be communicators don't really *know* what they want to say, and no attempt to polish writing skills will straighten out a hopeless case of muddled thinking. Yet as noted before, improving writing skills can also help clarify thinking.

Writer and editor Susan Mundale found that many executives are utterly surprised to learn how poorly their high-level employees write. "According to some estimates," Mundale writes, "more than two-thirds of the letters, memos and reports written in industry fail, in whole or in part, to meet their objectives."[1]

In government we've seen a parade of officials who use a stream of mysterious words, or words used mysteriously, that leave everyone guessing. William Safire, long a critic of language abuse, was one of the first to sound the alarm about General Alexander Haig. When quizzed about his stand on human rights at the hearings to confirm him as secretary of state, General Haig had replied, "There will be no de-emphasis but a change in priority." As Safire pointed out, how can a change from top priority *not* be a de-emphasis?

Seth Lipsky, writing in the *Wall Street Journal,* was also taken by Haig's mutilations of the English language. Speaking about guidelines for possible retribution to terrorists, Mr. Haig stated, "I said, I think, to somebody last night, that was consciously ambiguous, that statement, consciously ambiguous in the sense that any terrorist government or terrorist movement that is contemplating such actions I think knows clearly what we are speaking of." Haig went on, "Now, as you parcel it out in the context of individuals or separatist movements or independence movements, of course the problem is substantially different and the restraints and the ability to apply retaliatory action is sometimes not only constrained but uncertain. And so I caveat it that way."

The Nixon years produced an entirely new argot, including such memorable terms as *stonewalling* for "offering complete resistance" and *deep-sixing* for "burying the facts." During those years we became acquainted with *the bottom line, at this point in time,* and *time frame.*

The airline industry has developed its own language. If you've flown recently, you didn't fly in an airplane or even a jet. The airplane is referred to as "equipment," as in, "We are having some equipment problems and will be an hour behind schedule," or "The equipment hasn't arrived at the gate yet, thus the reason for this short delay."

Edwin Newman believes we can place a good deal of the blame for the current crisis squarely on the social sciences. He also gives appropriate credit to government and to the business world, particularly to advertising. But he believes that sociology and psychology have had a great influence on language and writing and have led people to express themselves in a more technical way: "They think it is expressive but it isn't. For example, they talk about *interpersonal relations* rather than personal relations, or, indeed, relations."[2]

Newman's concern is that the social sciences have invented a new language to describe concepts when the present language would have served well. When asked why, he replied, "It is self-importance and an attempt, on the part of those who use it, to convince themselves that what they are doing is important, and somehow difficult or abstruse, and that it takes some special training to understand it."[3]

Paul Woodring, who was education editor of *Saturday Review* during the 1960s, is critical of the educator as writer. "Educators seem to have difficulty avoiding the use of vogue words, euphemisms, and jargon."[4]

Vogue words are those that have become fashionable to use. *Competency-based education* is a vogue phrase. It means that students are able to do something when they finish a course or a degree. *Back to basics* is also a vogue phrase in education, despite the lack of general agreement about what the basics are.

Euphemisms are words or phrases invented to take the place of those considered more painful or embarrassing. We don't die, we "pass on." We talk about "gifted" children and "special education" when we mean some kids are smarter than others. We excuse ourselves to "visit the rest room."

Every field, every profession, has its jargon—special words to describe what it does and how it does it. Educators talk about "learning objectives" and "learning experiences" when they refer to what they are trying to do and how. Dentists talk about "caries" instead of cavities. Sailors say "head" when they mean toilet. Jargon as special language for special fields can perhaps be tolerated, but pseudo-jargon invites criticism. It is pretentious and designed solely to impress readers because it sounds technical and scientific. One editor I know says that when she translates educational jargon into English, the writers often sound foolish and simplistic because all they've done is paraphrase the obvious. Jargon words and phrases usually confuse rather than communicate. Worse, they make readers angry and sometimes cause automatic rejection of the writer's message.

Why do so many people have problems communicating, especially writing? Why are many apparently reluctant to try to improve their writing skills? Let's look at some of the common myths about writing.

Common Myths About Writing

1. *Writers are born, not made.* Many people believe that to become an acceptable writer, you must be born with a talent for writing. Talent is, of course, connected with writing, particularly if you wish to become a best-selling novelist or a nationally acclaimed poet or playwright. But fiction or poetry writing is one thing; understandable prose is another. Understandable prose requires basic writing skills that can be learned.

2. *Writing is not really very important in what one does.* Many people see writing as a minor matter compared with their other activities. If you're a student working on a research project, you may believe that gathering research material, compiling data, and manipulating them with a computer are the important activities. Writing up the research is viewed as the least important part of the entire process. Yet how you communicate your research is key to the entire project. If you can't explain what you have done and what you found out, the entire task could be a failure.

3. *Numbers are more important than words.* Since the advent of the computer, our society has become increasingly interested in numbers. Some would have us believe that everything worth communicating can be communicated with numbers. But the richness of communication required for most ideas can be accomplished only by the written word, no matter how adept we become with numbers. Numbers are important, but they can never replace words.

   4. *The world has become an audiovisual one. The written word is clearly on the wane.* When TV first flashed on in an electronic snowstorm, naysayers reported the demise of books and the written word. That simply has not happened. The written word has continued to hold its place in the world.

   5. *It takes a big vocabulary to write easily.* This myth implies that unless you have an above-average vocabulary, you have no hope of improving your writing skills. Rubbish. A good working vocabulary is helpful, to be sure. But a vocabulary laced with polysyllabic words is more often a detriment than an asset to the writer working on improving skills. Short, simple words and specific, down-to-earth language carry the strongest punch.

   6. *A long piece of writing is better than a short one.* This applies particularly to students who believe that the longer the term paper, the response to an essay question, or the thesis, the better. But the problem exists in the professional world too, where long reports and memos are gaining vogue. Although it may appear that a lengthy piece of writing requires more work than a short one, often the opposite is true. Assuming that it's thorough, the shorter piece requires more time. When Winston Churchill was invited to give a speech at a major political gathering, he was asked how long it would take him to prepare. He replied, "If my speech is two hours long, I can give it this afternoon, but if you are asking me to give a half hour speech, I will need a week to prepare, and if you only have time for five minutes, then I will need at least three weeks to prepare."

   Blaise Pascal, the seventeenth-century French philosopher, once wrote apologetically, "I have made this letter a little longer than usual because I lack the time to make it shorter."

   Short, concise writing has more impact than long, meandering writing. If someone doesn't know what to say, he or she usually takes several pages to say it. Working through exactly what you have to say is hard work, yet it usually results in a short, rather than a long, piece.

   7. *Writing skills are easily polished.* Visit any college bookstore. The shelves are lined with books on how to improve writing skills. Colleges sponsor writing labs for persons with writing problems, and many businesses conduct writing workshops for their employees. Unfortunately, the impression is that a book, a writing lab, or a writing workshop will provide the quick fix and solve a writing problem. Sometimes that is so, but not very often. Writing skills are not improved with one quick and easy lesson.

That is not to deny the importance of how-to books, labs, and workshops (more will be said about these resources in the following chapter). Improving writing skills, however, requires a commitment and a long-term learning plan. You don't become an expert golfer with one or two lessons; you don't learn swimming by reading a book or attending an hour session at the pool. You don't learn to play a musical instrument by attending a weekend crash course. Likewise, you don't improve writing skills without a long-range plan, commitment, and lots of practice.

8.   *Writers should never inject themselves into their writing.* That advice is often given in college writing classes and, at times, in writing workshops as well. Yet it is impossible to avoid including yourself in your writing. The facts you select to write about and the phrases you use are a reflection of you. You include some and discard others.

Unfortunately, many persons, particularly students, seem to think that "objective" writing means stringing together quotations with a few transitions stuck in between. This mindless mishmash is presented as objective writing by many students and, unfortunately, applauded by some professors.

Good writing starts with the writer's ideas. These ideas may be based on original research. They may be influenced and supported by the writing of others. But the ideas presented are the writer's. If the writer is not a part of the writing, he or she should merely pass out a list of the quoted sources so the reader can go directly to them.

9.   *Professional wordsmiths will correct any writing problems.* A wordsmith is an editor-writer who takes tangled ideas and sloppy writing and works them over until they are understandable. Many businesses, industries, and governmental agencies have such editor-writers available. They are used as a crutch. Those responsible for writing reports, proposals, and the like take their raw material to the editor-writer and expect the beginning glimmers of an idea to be polished into professional prose. It is asking the impossible of the wordsmith. Not only must the wordsmith be an expert editor-writer, but he or she must be a mind reader as well.

Wordsmiths can play an important role in the writing process. But they shouldn't be expected to create the ideas the author wants to communicate.

A common practice a few years ago was for college students to buy prewritten, professionally prepared term papers on almost any topic. Students could even specify whether they wanted an A paper or a B paper; naturally, the A paper was more expensive than the B paper.

Writers must develop their own ideas and present them in the best possible way. The editor-writer has a role in making last-minute corrections, finding flaws in grammar and spelling, and sometimes even pointing out shortcomings in the writer's logic. But it is the responsibility of the writer to create the writing and see it through the various stages of revision.

10. *All writers must consciously work at developing a writing style.* Many writers are concerned about style. They may have heard about the Hemingway style, the Fitzgerald style, the Michener style, and wonder what kind of style they should develop.

Don't emulate a writing style or even consciously try to develop one. Just write, following the best principles of the craft. The kind of writing you do *is* your style. You can find out what your style is by looking at your writing when it's finished. But it's better to forget about writing style and try to communicate your ideas in the most concise way possible. Your writing style will take care of itself.

What Does It Take to Write Better?

After spending many years working with returning students and teaching writing workshops for business and professional people and others, I've come in contact with several hundred students. Many of them have become good writers. The following are some characteristics that they and other good writers possess:

• A fundamental interest in words. Good writers are people who love words, their shapes, their sounds, and the vast variety of meanings they can communicate. Successful writers are interested in the fine distinctions and subtle shades of meaning between words. They are able to hear the *rhythm* of words, which words go together and which do not. They are interested enough in words to search for their histories occasionally, for in this way one comes to really know a word.

• A knowledge of the subject to be communicated. Sometimes the very process of writing can help you discover what you do and do not know about a topic.

• Technical writing skills. To be a successful carpenter, one needs to know how to use a saw and a square, how to read blueprints, and a hundred other technical skills. Before much of anything can be built, these skills must be present and polished. It's true for the successful writer too. How to write a sentence and a paragraph, how to choose which word to use and when, how to spell, how to punctuate, how to do research, how to organize ideas—all are technical skills essential for good writing.

• Creativity as well as discipline. The development of thinking creatively and the necessity of disciplining creative ideas into formats and structures that communicate will be discussed later. For now, let it suffice to say that both creativity and disciplined forms are necessary. Often the student or business writer will write with an excess of disciplined form but little creativity. That leads to technically accurate but boring writing, writing without new ideas or excitement.

Discipline must also be looked at in another sense. It takes a good deal of personal discipline to write words on paper. Writing is not an activity for spare moments nestled between appointments. Time must be set aside for writing (at least an hour each time). It takes discipline to do this, particularly if the project requires several writing sessions to complete. It's far easier to find something else to do rather than sit down and write.

• The ability to see the relationship of the whole to its parts. A successful writer is able to see the totality of a piece of writing and to ask such questions as, What is this report (or term paper or proposal) trying to accomplish? At the same time, the successful writer can see the relationship of the many pieces that make up a writing project—the various sections, anecdotes, and so on—and how they relate to the overall purpose of the writing. Many people can see the pieces and handle them well, but they run into difficulty when they try to relate the pieces to one another and to the entire writing project. Sometimes, though, a person needs to begin writing before the various relationships become clear.

Writing Log

In the following chapter, you'll discover how to analyze your writing skills as well as how to map out a long-range plan to improve them. To begin your improvement program, you'll need some writing tasks.

Several writing exercises are included in this book. The first is a Writing Log, a notebook to keep track of what you're doing to improve your writing skills. More important, you can use the log to record your reactions to what you're doing. You'll discover insights about yourself and your writing that you didn't know you had. Frustrations and disappointments can be expressed in an easy, private way. You can also use your Writing Log to express your future plans for writing activities. And by looking back in your log, you can see evidence of your progress as you report the successes and failures of your writing efforts.

Besides being a record of your progress, the log is in itself a writing exercise. *To improve your writing skills, you must write.* There is no other way. Simply reading about improving skills or hearing someone talk about it is not enough. Writing is exactly like other skills—playing football, playing the piano, swimming—in that it must be practiced to be improved. Of course, you practice writing at work or as part of your educational assignments. But the Writing Log offers you one more opportunity to practice. The pressure is off when you're writing in the log because it's for your eyes only. I strongly urge you to begin a Writing Log as part of the process for improving your writing skills.

EXERCISES

For your Writing Log, choose a looseleaf binder so copies of outside writing and filled-in forms that are suggested by other exercises in this book can be included. Begin your Writing Log by answering the following questions:

1. Why do you want to improve your writing skills?
2. What have others told you about your writing? Be specific.
3. Which of the myths about writing and writers did you believe? Do you still believe them and, if so, why?

NOTES

1. Susan Mundale, "Why More CEOs Are Mandating Listening and Writing Training," *Training: The Magazine of Human Resources Development,* vol. l7, no. 10, October 1980.
2. Martin L. Gross, ed., *Between the Lines: Book Digest Interviews with Best Selling Authors, 1974–1979* (New York: Book Digest, 1980), p. 38.
3. Ibid.
4. Paul Woodring, "Writing About Education," *Phi Delta Kappan,* vol. 62, no. 7, March 1981, p. 500.

Chapter 2

Developing a Learning Plan for Improving Writing Skills

How can you improve your writing skills? Begin with a personal learning plan that you develop and carry out. A learning plan has five components that must be determined:

1. What you want or need to know
2. How you plan to learn (reading, attending courses, personal consultation, etc.)
3. When you want to learn
4. What constraints may hinder you and how you plan to overcome them
5. Whether you are learning what you want to know

Deciding What You Want or Need to Know

This is the first step in developing a learning plan. To find out what you want or need to know, answer the following questions:

What writing responsibilities do you have? Depending on your status, you may need to write term papers, essay exams, book reports, memos, reports, or proposals. You may also want your writing published, either in article or in book form.

What writing skills do you need to carry out these tasks? To answer this question, turn to the writing skills inventory (Appendix 1), where skills necessary for various writing tasks are listed. If your writing tasks have specific requirements that go beyond the inventory, list those additional requirements at the bottom of the skills inventory.

What writing skills do you now have? Complete the writing skills inventory and check your ability level for each skill: weak, fair, or strong. Once you've done this, give a sample of your writing to a friend or a colleague at work and ask him or her to appraise your perception of your writing skills honestly. You may believe your skills are greater than they are, or conversely, you may believe that some skills are inadequate when they are not. If any of the terms in the writing skills inventory are unfamiliar to you, you can find explanations of them elsewhere in the book by checking the Index.

Which skills need improvement? Compare the writing tasks you need with your inventory of writing skills. It should be evident which writing skills need improvement. Some skills you may wish to work on immediately; others you may delay for a time. Turn to the writing skills learning plan (Appendix 1) and list the writing skills you want to work on in the order you wish to work on them.

Planning How You Will Learn

Once you know which writing skills you want to improve, you're ready to decide how to go about improving them. To help you decide, here are several learning opportunities and a brief discussion of what you can expect from each.

Resource Books on Writing

Studying this book and others can be an excellent way to improve your writing skills. Chapter 14 includes a list of several books about writing, divided into various categories. To gain most from resource books on writing, however, you must be aware of the writing skills you're trying to develop. You must also learn to become an active reader.

To read a writing skills book actively, first ask yourself specific questions such as, How do I make my writing more readable? How do I get an article published? What are the techniques for avoiding sexist writing? Look for specific answers to your questions.

If you own the book, underline key words or phrases, or use a yellow marking pen. It's usually better to do this after you have read through the material once. Write summary words in the margins or put an asterisk beside each important word or phrase. You may also write questions in the margins and make summary statements at the end of sections or chapters.

If the book is not yours, take notes. Make sure the notes are more than just sentences and paragraphs you've copied from the book. *Think* about what you are reading and writing. Carry on a mental discussion with the author. Relate what you read to your own experience and note this. Rewrite the author's headings into statements that summarize what he or she is saying. Make a list of the main ideas the author is offering. Read only those parts of the book that relate most directly to your learning plan. Remember, you are in charge of your learning, which means *you* decide which parts of a book you will read. Occasionally, though, you will find an author who writes about something you haven't thought of before. It's important to learn new areas you hadn't planned for, so don't let your learning plan become something from which you cannot deviate.

Correspondence Courses

Correspondence courses are available from private concerns, colleges, and universities. Contact the college or university in your community for information about correspondence courses. Also, check such publications as *Writer's Digest* for advertising about correspondence courses for writers.

Check carefully before signing up for a correspondence course. Determine the answers to these questions:

Do you really need all the content of the course? Or are there several areas of the course in which you are already proficient?

Is the correspondence course worth the money you will spend? Only you can answer this question. The costs of correspondence courses vary considerably. Usually the courses offered by colleges and universities are less expensive than those offered by commercial concerns, but not always. Comparison-shop. Try to learn the names of some people who have taken the course you're considering and ask what they thought of it and whether they believed it was worth the money.

Who are the instructors? Are they writers who can help you with your problems? Are they experienced people, or are they inexperienced students who are earning a few dollars by working for the correspondence program?

What contacts will you have with the instructors? Will your only contact be through the brief comments made at the end of an assignment you turn in? Will you have the opportunity to talk to your instructor by phone? Can you write letters to your instructor that go beyond the written assignments?

How many people who sign up for the course complete it? A serious shortcoming of many home-study correspondence courses is that students do not complete assignments and drop out, yet they often are charged the entire fee.

Does the correspondence program use other approaches to contact students besides the mail? Are there opportunities for the students to meet face to face at some time? Do the instructors or others routinely call students to ask about progress and answer any questions they may have?

Does the course offer more than written materials? Modern approaches to correspondence study often combine tape-recorded materials with written materials, providing more active formats to maintain the interest of the student.

Are the written assignments returned promptly? This can be a problem if you want to move quickly through a program and are held up because your instructor delays returning the materials to you.

Does the instructor give you accurate feedback about how you are doing? True, you want to be praised, but you signed up for the course to improve. To improve, you need to know honestly how well you are doing.

Do you receive comments from the same instructor each time or from different instructors depending on the lessons submitted? Usually you will benefit most by working with the same instructor throughout the course. By working with the same instructor, you can develop something that approaches a teacher-learner relationship, which can be an important part of learning. The instructor, over time, can learn to know you and your work and can be more helpful to you and your writing problems.

Formal Writing Courses

In a formal writing course, students and instructor meet face to face over an extended period of time—from six to eighteen weeks or more. Colleges and universities usually offer two kinds of formal courses: credit and noncredit. Noncredit courses often offer Continuing Education Units (CEUs) as a record of attendance. Writing courses may also be offered by YMCAs and YWCAs, vocational schools, and other providers.

The same questions about correspondence courses also apply to formal face-to-face courses:

Are the instructors experienced writers and qualified teachers?

Is the content of the course in tune with your learning plan? Don't depend on college catalog descriptions for accurate statements about a course. Contact the instructor for a copy of the course outline to be sure it has the content you want.

What does it cost? Courses with nearly identical content will vary widely in costs, depending on the offering agency or institution. Of course, you must balance cost with the quality of the content and the instructor.

Who takes the course? Ask the instructor for names of former students. Contact a few of them and ask about the content, the instructor, and their reasons for taking the course. Are they at the same level as you? Are they published authors trying to hone advanced skills? Or are they people who have never written and think about writing only as a hobby? A few of these last two will present no problems, but if either group is in the majority, you could have a less than profitable experience.

What teaching approach does the instructor use? Some instructors find teaching writing courses a personal ego trip; they discuss their various writing achievements rather than show concern for students' writing progress. A teaching format useful to those interested in improving their writing skills is one in which students can raise questions of the instructor and receive critical comment about their writing from both the instructor and other students in the class. The instructor should be available for individual consultation about your writing problems before or after classes or by appointment between classes. Sometimes your particular problem is not discussed during class, and you need the opportunity to obtain the answers to your questions.

Are reference materials provided? Does the instructor give you suggestions about additional readings that may help you with organization, research, grammar, or whatever your problem may be?

Does the instructor give you specific critical comments and not general statements such as, "This needs more work," or "The lead paragraph is weak"? You should expect and receive specific comment about what improvements are necessary in your writing.

Are the classes offered at times convenient to your work schedule? Many institutions offer classes in the late afternoon, in the evening, and on weekends to accommodate those who work full time. Some institutions also offer courses using media such as audiotapes, videotapes, and workbooks.

Writers' Conferences

A writers' conference is usually a two-day to two-week intensive experience for writers and instructors. In contrast to a course, which usually meets for a couple of hours once a week for several weeks, a conference meets every day and often every evening as well. Usually several areas of interest, such as article writing and nonfiction book writing, are offered for study. Different instructors teach the classes. (See chapter 14 for a brief listing of annual writers' conferences and additional sources of information.)

Some authors argue that writers' conferences are a waste of time and that a budding writer could gain more by staying home and writing. For some writers, that may be true. But for many, a writers' conference provides an opportunity to rub shoulders with other writers who are struggling and have many of the same problems. There also is the inspiration that comes from meeting authors who have done well (though that can be a frustration too). Most people who attend writers' conferences return home enthusiastic and highly motivated to develop their writing skills. For some, the motivation remains until they attend the next writers' conference, when they are once more recharged. For others, the motivation evaporates when they return home.

Some questions about writers' conferences to consider before deciding to attend:

Are you sufficiently interested in being published? Because the emphasis of writers' conferences is on just that. Also, most of those who attend writers' conferences (though many would not admit it) are striving to become full-time professional writers. Are you interested in studying in that type of atmosphere?

Who are the instructors? Very likely the people leading classes at a conference are successfully published writers, editors, or others actively involved in the business of publishing. Just because an instructor has a recognized name as a writer does not mean he or she is a good teacher. Get the names of people who have attended the conference from the conference director and ask them about the various instructors.

Can you afford both the conference cost and the travel cost to the conference? Will you gain enough from the experience to make it worth the cost?

What is the philosophy of the conference? Some conferences have an elitist philosophy, admitting only those who are advanced in their writing abilities. Others, like the Rhinelander School of Arts in Wisconsin, will admit anyone who pays the fee.

How does the conference operate? Will you only hear lectures from notable authors, or will you also have the opportunity to participate in workshop groups where your writing and the writing of others is critiqued by your instructor and other students in the class?

Teacherless Classes

Let's say there are four or five of you who are interested in improving your writing skills. You may all be in school. You may all work for the same firm. Or you may all live on the same side of town and discover you are interested in doing something about your writing skills. You could organize your own writing class, and it would cost you essentially nothing.

One advantage of a teacherless class, besides the no-cost feature, is the honest feedback you can receive from a small group of people who read your material and comment on it. When trying to improve writing skills, it's most useful to get an honest appraisal of how your writing sounds, what it says, and whether it's understandable, boring, interesting, or effective. A second advantage is that you are *motivated* to write. If you know you must produce something for your colleagues to review and discuss, you're more apt to do it.

Here's how to set up a teacherless class. Talk to four or five other people who are interested in improving their writing skills and who would contribute to a small group. Make a commitment to meet for six months, say once a month for $2^{1}/_{2}$ to 3 hours, and to write something for each of the meetings. It could be something written specifically for the meeting, a proposal written for work, or a school term paper or seminar report.

Each member of the group should send to the others a copy of his or her writing at least a week before the group meets. At the meeting, allow time to discuss each person's writing. If you're holding three-hour meetings and there are five people in your group, each person has more than half an hour.

To gain a sense of how others react to the rhythm of the writing, have each person read aloud—preferably twice—some of what he or she has written. The first time, the group gets an overall reaction; the second time, they are able to detect more specific problems.

Peter Elbow[1] offers some suggestions about the kind of feedback to give the writers in the group after you have both read their material and listened to it. He suggests you first give the writer your reaction to the piece—how did it affect you as a reader or listener? Which words or phrases caught your attention? Which words or phrases sounded weak or out of place?

Second, summarize the writing. Give the main ideas back to the writer. If possible, summarize the point of the piece in a single sentence. Choose one word from the piece that best summarizes what's been said.

Third, tell the writer what happened to you as you read or listened. Elbow says this is best done in the form of a story: first this happened, and then this.

Elbow offers some dos and don'ts for critiquing writing in the teacherless class:

1. Emphasize reaction to the writing.

2. Read the material twice; read it out loud twice if written copies are not provided. A sensible critique cannot be made if the group hasn't had a chance to interact with the material.

3. Encourage the group to give specific reactions to specific parts of the writing.

4. Emphasize how you felt about the writing as well as what you understood from it.

5. As the writer who is receiving comments, don't argue with a person's reactions. Listen quietly, even though you may be uncomfortable.

6. As the writer who is receiving comments, don't apologize for what you have written or how you have written it.

7. Don't let one person dominate the discussion. Encourage all to respond to the piece of writing under consideration. An advantage of the teacherless class is that the writer receives reactions from several different people. All must have an opportunity.[2]

Writing Laboratories

If you're a student, you likely have access to a writing laboratory on your campus. Such laboratories, often sponsored by college or university English departments, are designed for students with particular kinds of writing problems. Instructors refer students to the writing laboratory for help. As part of the referral, an instructor specifies what writing problems the student has. The instructor may check such problems as sentence structure, paragraph structure, organization of material, factual material, vocabulary, and overall style.

The writing laboratories at some universities offer individual instruction to students as well as other learning opportunities. They may sponsor noncredit writing courses to improve writing skills and assist with course-related writing. These courses meet from four to six hours and deal with specific topics, such as basic and advanced sentence structure and mechanics, revision techniques, principles of organization, literature papers, and essay exams. Some writing laboratories also provide computer terminals for students who want drills on sentence structure, as well as cassette lessons on spelling and vocabulary.

Hired Critics

Writing magazines carry ads for people who will read and comment on your writing for a fee. Two kinds of ads appear. First are those that offer a careful reading with suggestions for improvement. For example, *Writer's Digest* offers a criticism service that claims it "thoroughly examines your work through the discerning eye of an editor and takes the time required to pinpoint the areas that are keeping the piece out of print. We proudly offer you:

"Manuscript Review by Professional Writers Who Know What an Editor Looks For: They've Been There

"Advice on Where to Submit Your Material From a Staff That Has Their Fingers on the Pulse of the Market."

The fees charged for these services may be $30 for an article up to 3,000 words and a minimum of $125 for a book outline with sample chapter.

A second kind of ad offering criticism comes under the guise of literary agents. An ad asks whether you would like to be represented by an agent who can sell your material to a big New York publisher. Many fledgling writers have heard about the importance of literary agents (see chapter 13) and so submit material to the firms that advertise, with the hope of quick publication by a major publishing house. Often the ad will also say there is no charge for reading. But read the ad completely, and you'll see a comment about services for a fee. The free reading does not include criticism, analysis, or editorial work of any kind. Once you submit your material for the "free reading," you're told that editorial services and rewriting are necessary, and a fee is quoted. If a book manuscript is involved, that fee is often several thousand dollars. And if you read even further, you see that all the work is done on author's speculation, which means there is no assurance the material will ever be published.

Another kind of hired critic is one you find in your community: a professional journalist, an English teacher adept at manuscript criticism, or a professional editor who would be willing to read your material and offer criticism for a fee. This is an excellent way to receive outside criticism, particularly if you've found a qualified person. Whereas you may pay several thousand dollars for a book appraisal when you answer a national ad, you may pay a few hundred dollars for professional criticism right at home. And you will often receive much more for your money because the criticism will be face to face; you can ask your critic questions.

Working with a Friend

You can often receive important criticism of your writing by work-ing with a friend whom you trust and respect. If the friend you choose is someone who is also attempting to improve his or her writing skills, criticism can be done on an exchange basis.

One caution, though: The two of you should discuss what kind of criticism is expected. Ask the friend such things as, Have I left out important areas of content that should be included? Do you under-stand what I'm trying to say? Is the tone right? What kind of feeling do you get when you read this material? Are there obvious errors in how certain words or technical terms are used? Have I made some obvious errors in English?

By giving your friend a list of questions such as these, your chances of receiving specific comments are much greater than if you say only, "React to this material." With that kind of request, the response is often "Sounds good to me" or perhaps "Something about it wasn't just right." Neither of these two reactions is particu-larly helpful. To make changes in your writing, you need *specific* comments. And specific comments come in reaction to specific questions.

An obvious advantage of working with a friend who lives in your community (you can also work with friends through the mail or over the telephone) is the ability to talk face to face and probe what he or she really has to suggest about your writing.

Writing Magazines

Two prominent writing magazines particularly designed for writers seeking publication are the *Writer* and *Writer's Digest* (addresses of both are in chapter 14). Both are monthly publications, and both carry articles useful to the writer trying to improve writing skills. In addition to articles that range from how to improve your spelling to how to interview, and from writing lead paragraphs to submitting a book proposal, both magazines carry lists of publishers who purchase manuscripts for publication.

These magazines can be useful to your writing improvement pro-gram for several reasons. A person trying to improve writing skills learns that he or she is not alone in this endeavor and that it is indeed possible to improve. Although most of the articles do not go into depth about a particular writing problem, it is often possible to gain valuable new ideas and shortcuts to deal with writing problems.

For those interested in publishing their writing, particularly book manuscripts, *Publishers Weekly* is an excellent magazine found in many libraries. It includes the most up-to-date information available about such topics as the kinds of books selling now, industry trends, and prospects.

Local Writers' Clubs

In many communities writers have organized clubs. These can be useful organizations for improving writing skills, particularly if you're interested in publication. If you can't find others to join you in a teacherless class, a writers' club could serve the same purpose.

National Writers' Groups

See chapter 14 for a sampling of these organizations. Most sponsor annual conferences and workshops to help members improve writing skills. Their emphasis is on writing for publication.

Reading Programs

A shortcoming of many who want to improve their writing skills is the lack of a solid reading program. Reading and writing go hand in hand. Reading good books contributes to good writing. Much of the writing you read today is terrible. It is jargon laden, obtuse, and pompous, often exhibiting many of the faults described earlier. And that is the writing you have for a model. To become a better writer, it helps to have writing models that are exemplary, that demonstrate the writing skills you are attempting to achieve. I encourage nonfiction writing students to read novels and short stories with an eye for the writing skills used.

Questions to consider when reading are these:

How does the author use words? What different shades of meaning do the words carry?

What devices does the author use to keep you reading, to keep you from falling asleep or putting down the book?

How does the author use tone, rhythm, sentence structure, and organization?

What research has the author done? How has the author incorporated research material into the narrative so that it flows and is interesting to read?

What feelings does the author evoke in you as you read?

There is not sufficient space here to list books that are examples of good writing. Some authors to consider reading are John Steinbeck, Eudora Welty, F. Scott Fitzgerald, Virginia Woolf, Mortimer Adler, Bertrand Russell, Dorothy Sayers, John Updike, and Doris Lessing.

Making a Decision

With twelve different approaches to improving your writing skills, you're probably wondering how to choose those that will be of most help. To decide, it helps to look at the way you prefer to learn. We do not all prefer the same approaches to learning. This chart may help you decide on your preferred learning approach.

When I am trying to learn something, I prefer—	Always	Sometimes	Never
working by myself			
working with others			
working at my own pace			
working at the pace of a group			
learning by lecture			

Some of us enjoy combinations of the above; we may prefer to learn certain things by ourselves and other things in groups. Or we may enjoy different paces depending on what we are trying to learn. But in most instances, an adult has a preferred approach to learning.

If you checked that you enjoy working by yourself at your own pace, you would probably enjoy the following learning activities:

> Resource books on writing
> Correspondence courses
> Writing magazines
> Reading programs

If you enjoy working in the company of another person or a small group, the following learning activities would fit:

> Formal writing courses
> Teacherless classes
> Writing laboratories
> Hired critics
> Working with a friend
> Local writers' clubs

If the stimulation of a large group enhances your learning, you should select from these:

>Writers' conferences
>National writers' groups

There is no "best way" to learn how to improve your writing skills. For most learners, some combination of the learning activities mentioned above works well.

Deciding When You Want to Learn

Finding time for an organized learning program is a problem for almost everyone. For your learning program to succeed, you must organize your time so the learning plan receives some priority. Unless you're careful about this, your well-intentioned learning plan will start with enthusiasm and die for lack of attention. You must not only take charge of what you're going to learn and the way you're going to learn it. You must also decide *when* you're going to learn it.

To figure out a time schedule, first decide in which learning activities you want to participate. If you decide on a formal writing course or a writers' conference, you must obviously adjust your schedule to fit the time for the course or conference. But if you want to emphasize a teacherless class, working with a friend, a correspondence course, or reading writing magazines and books on writing, you must select a time in your schedule to do it. Because these activities are more flexible in their time requirements, you probably think it will be easier to work them into your schedule. Some say, "I'll do these things when I have time."

Unfortunately, unless a specific time is planned for the activity, it is not done and soon forgotten. One way to overcome this difficulty is to keep a time inventory and then work out a specific time when you will work on your writing skills learning plan.

Time Inventory

Using the weekly time inventory worksheet (Appendix 1) for a week, keep a record of how you spend your time from early morning until you go to bed at night. Write down the time you're working, commuting to work, spending time with your family, bowling, golfing, or whatever recreation you participate in. Keep a record of it all, and then look for patterns. Are there certain activities you can adjust that would give you a minimum of an hour, preferably two hours, to work on writing skills improvement each day (or at least twice a week)?

A Weekly Plan

Once you've completed the time inventory and determined your activity patterns, figure how you can adjust your time schedule. It's better to have shorter periods of time scheduled throughout the week than to block out Sunday afternoon or Saturday morning to work on your learning plan. Using the weekly time plan (Appendix 1), map a week's activities, including the hours you'll spend on writing skills improvement.

Self-discipline is the key to a self-directed learning plan that is made up of activities such as reading and correspondence course work. There will be days when you won't feel like working on a correspondence course, or working with a friend who is criticizing your work, or doing whatever activity you've planned for yourself. However, once you have set aside a time for working on your plan, stick to it. (Many musicians set a certain time every day for practice and do it day after day, week after week, whether they feel like practicing or not.)

If you do become a full-time or even a part-time professional writer, you'll discover that successful writers are those who are highly disciplined. They write every day, whether they feel like writing or not, whether they are inspired or not. They write.

The same can be said for learning, particularly learning about how to improve writing skills. The same skills necessary for good writing—skills of disciplined work—apply to self-directed learning.

Determining Constraints and How to Overcome Them

Once you've decided what, how, and when you want to learn, you need to think about possible constraints and how to overcome them. What will a six-month learning plan cost—in money, time, energy, and relationships with spouse, family, and friends? Learning is hard work, particularly if you develop a learning plan on top of all the other activities in which you are involved.

Money can be a constraint. But careful planning can help you avoid major financial costs. A reading program using the library can be done for essentially no cost. Working with a friend or with a teacherless class costs no money. If you're careful in choosing conferences, workshops, and formal courses, you can find those that come closest to meeting your needs for minimal financial cost.

Don't overlook the potential costs in relationships. Developing a self-directed learning plan, even a low-budget one, must involve those who are close to you. They must be involved in the planning stages and the time scheduling discussed above. What does your spouse think of the idea of developing a long-range learning plan that includes spending money on a writing course that meets every Wednesday night, the night you and your spouse usually go bowling? What does your spouse think of your plan if he or she wants to save money for a trip instead of a course?

If your spouse's lack of interest in your learning plan is a possible constraint, what will you do about it? How can you involve your spouse so that he or she will be supportive? One way is to ask whether your spouse would be willing to help you with some of the writing projects you plan to do.

Your work or school schedule can be a constraint. Your own energy level can be a constraint. Unavailability of resources can be a constraint. If you live in a small town, your local public library may not have many of the books you want to include as part of your reading program. Although the books are likely available on an inter-library loan, such procedures often take time.

On your learning plan form, list the constraints you're likely to face in carrying out your learning plan and indicate how you will overcome them.

Assessing Your Learning

When you've completed the learning plan, reflect on your writing progress. The Writing Log is an excellent device for determining the progress you've made. The improvement in the writing within the log is itself a measure of writing skills progress.

Compare the writing projects you do at work or the assignments you do as a student with those you did before you began your learning project. Feedback from your teacherless writing group, a friend, members of a writing club, your spouse, or anyone who has seen your writing efforts over some length of time is useful. These people can show you areas of improvement and areas where improvement is still necessary.

Go back to the writing skills inventory that you completed at the beginning of your writing skills improvement plan and fill it out again, comparing what you checked then with what you perceive to be your present skills. As a follow-up, you may wish to develop another learning plan.

EXERCISES

1. Add copies of the completed writing skills inventory, learning plan, and time schedules to your Writing Log.
2. Keep a record of your progress in following the learning plan in your Writing Log.
3. Compare the writing projects you do at work or the assignments you do as a student with those you did before you began your learning project. Write in your log the feedback you want to remember.

NOTES

1. Peter Elbow, *Writing Without Teachers* (New York: Oxford University Press, 1973).
2. Ibid., pp. 85–127.

Chapter 3

Finding the Facts

If you're going to write, you've got to have something to write about. Some writers, especially students, often drown in facts. The term papers, theses, and reports they write list fact upon fact (usually quoted material) with no attempt to provide a context for understanding the facts or to relate them to the writer's experience. On the other hand, other writers often lack facts. One of the basic reasons much work offered for publication is rejected is shallow research and lack of facts.

Your Own Experience

Your experience is one of your most valuable assets and an important source of information for your writing. Personal experience obviously should not be your sole source of "facts," but don't overlook it either.

Keeping a diary or a journal is a way to record your everyday experiences. In a journal you can comment on an article or book you're reading, someone you've just met, a committee meeting that impressed or disturbed you, something your children did, changes in the weather, and so on. Some people copy quotations with references into their journals so they can find them later if they need to. A journal is a good place to record not only the happenings in your life but also your reactions. A record of your feelings can be as important as what you experience.

Clipping File

Al Nelson, a full-time free-lance writer and part-time writing teacher for the University of Wisconsin–Extension, introduced me to the idea of a clipping file. Al reads a newspaper or magazine with scissors in hand. When he comes upon an article or a news story that he thinks may be of some use to him someday, he cuts it out and files it. He has an elaborate system of folders in which he files the clippings according to topic areas.

How might this work for you? Let's say you have an interest in the left side–right side brain research that has become popular in recent years. Every time you run across an article about this topic, cut it out and tuck it away. There may come a time when you want to report on this topic in an office newsletter, a term paper, or an article for publication. The clipping file then becomes a good, handy source of information.

Or let's assume you're a student working on a graduate degree and one of the requirements is to carry out an original research project. Let's also assume you have the idea for the research project in mind but it isn't well developed. As you read textbooks, journals, newspapers, and popular magazines and come upon articles that relate to your research, either clip or photocopy the material to add to your clipping file. This will save you the hours of time it would take to go back and find material that you vaguely remember.

The Library

The obvious source of facts for most people is the library. No matter who you are or what you do, the library is the place to begin when searching for factual material.

Kinds of Libraries

Almost every community, even a very small rural one, has a public library. With today's interlibrary loan systems, the small public library can be your entry to almost every imaginable kind of material.

In larger communities public libraries have more materials and services at hand. For instance, in addition to the regular book stacks and the reference section, libraries often have large periodical sections, record collections, and films, slides, and video cassettes that circulate. Larger libraries also have reference librarians on duty to help you find particular information, often with only a phone call.

A second kind of library is a research library, usually found on a college or university campus. Sometimes access is a problem for those who are not enrolled as students, but many research libraries have worked out arrangements so nonstudents can use the materials.

Research libraries have the specialized materials that researchers need and are valuable sources for anyone who wishes to explore a particular topic in depth. Research libraries subscribe to hundreds of scholarly journals in which up-to-date research is reported from throughout the world. Reference books are procured with the researcher in mind.

A third kind of library found in many communities is the historical library. Today even smaller communities often have historical libraries connected with local museums or historical societies. For those writing projects involving historical facts, a historical library is a good place to start for newspapers, reports, government surveys, statistics, and, depending on the size of the library, a vast array of other source materials.

Contents of a Library

You can usually find the following in every library: a card catalog, reference works, an area for reading, periodicals, the book stacks, and an audiovisual section. In a small community library, all of these may be in one room. At a large university, more than one building may be required to house these sections. The first thing to do is acquaint yourself with the library or the libraries in your community and find out how they are laid out.

For most research projects, start with the card catalog. Here you'll find three kinds of cards: author cards, title cards, and subject cards. If you know the author of a work, you naturally start with the author card. But if you have a subject yet don't know specific authors or titles, start with the subject cards.

Increasingly, libraries are putting their card catalogs on computers. This allows you to search the card catalog from a computer terminal some distance from the library to determine all the books the library has on a particular topic, who the authors are, and whether the books are checked out.

You may also begin your research in the periodical section of the library. Start with the *Readers' Guide to Periodical Literature.* Here you can find out what has been published in periodicals on the topic you are researching. Many libraries have bound copies of periodicals you can use.

You could begin a research project with a computer search. Most large libraries, particularly research libraries, have direct ties to computer banks around the country. By typing into a computer terminal certain descriptors—words that describe what you are researching—you can find out who has completed research on your topic and can often read on the terminal screen an abstract of the research. When you see research that seems applicable to your project, you can order printed copies of the abstract or even the entire research report. All of this, of course, is for a fee, including a fee for the initial computer search. However, the computer search can save you hours of poring over indexes and back issues of research journals, particularly if your research project involves use of the kind of information found in research journals.

Browsing the book stacks is still another way to begin a research project. Go to the card catalog and obtain the name and call number of a book on your subject. Once you've found the book in the stacks, look at the other books in the same section. You may find several others relevant to your research with this kind of informal browsing.

It helps to know something about how library books are cataloged when browsing the stacks. Libraries use one of two classification systems, the Dewey Decimal Classification or the Library of Congress system. Detailed information about these classification systems can be found in the library research references in chapter 14.

The reference section of the library is also a good place to find answers to many research questions. Here are some reference books you should find in most libraries.

• Dictionaries. One of the most valuable, particularly if you're interested in the histories of words, is the *Oxford English Dictionary,* which comes in twelve volumes. It's often useful to check more than one dictionary for definitions of words. Two other good unabridged dictionaries are *Webster's Third New International Dictionary* and *Funk and Wagnalls New Standard Dictionary of the English Language.*

• Encyclopedias. Although they are almost always somewhat out of date (many produce yearbooks to correct this problem), they are useful sources of general information. Two commonly found in libraries are *Encyclopaedia Britannica* and *Encyclopedia Americana.*

- Indexes. These guides help you find information on a variety of topics. The *Readers' Guide to Periodical Literature* is one example. Other valuable indexes are the quarterly *Biography Index,* an index of biographical material appearing in current books and periodicals, and the biennial *Who's Who in America,* the standard source on notable living Americans.

- Yearbooks and almanacs. Collections of miscellaneous facts and statistical information. Two such references are *Information Please Almanac* and *Statistical Abstract of the United States,* an annual digest of data collected by agencies of the United States government.

- Books of quotations. Who had something to say on the topic you are researching, and how was it said? Check *Bartlett's Familiar Quotations.*

- Atlases. These, of course, are bound collections of maps, such as the *Rand McNally Cosmopolitan World Atlas* and the *Encyclopaedia Britannica World Atlas International.*

Permissions

As a researcher using the library and copying material from re-·search articles and books, you must be aware of copyrights and permissions. There are few problems if you are writing term papers, reports, theses, or dissertations; for these you do not have to obtain permission for material that you quote verbatim (you must always give credit, though). Permission is also not usually required when you quote copyrighted material for critical reviews, scholarship, and academic research. But if you're interested in publishing your work, either as an article or a book, you must know about permissions.

The term *fair use* means using published copyrighted material in such a way that you do not need to obtain permission for its use. One aspect of fair use concerns the length of the quotation. A rule of thumb some book publishers follow: Quoting or paraphrasing more than 125 to 150 words of copyrighted material requires written permission for its use. Fewer than 125 to 150 words is usually considered fair use.

Whether you should write for permission also depends on the kind of material you wish to quote. If you are quoting even one line from a poem or a song, you must seek permission. If you include a published cartoon, table, or chart in your book, you must ask for permission to use it.

How do you obtain permission? First, obtain the name and address of the publisher of the work you wish to quote. (If the book itself does not include the publisher's address, look it up in either *Literary Market Place* or *Writer's Market*. Both these references should be available on your library's reference shelf.) Then write to the publisher, calling your request to the attention of the permissions editor. Sending a self-addressed, stamped envelope speeds up the process. Appendix 2 contains a sample permissions request.

You may be required to pay for permission to use materials, sometimes several hundred dollars. Whether you are required to pay and, if so, the amount you pay often depend on the intended use and audience of the material. If you're writing a book that will be widely distributed, you usually have to pay for permission.

People

People can be a valuable source of research information. Using people as a resource involves several decisions, including who you want to contact and what approach you're going to use to interview them—personal visit, telephone, or letter. Of course, you'll also need to spend considerable time determining the kinds of information you want from other people. And once you have the information, you must then decide what you have, whether it is accurate, and how it relates to other information you have. Using people to get information is not an easy process. But it can be a valuable one.

Personal Interviews

If you've had training in the social sciences, you likely know some social science research approaches, particularly survey approaches. The social sciences have developed elaborate sampling systems to obtain opinions and other information from a relatively small number of people who represent larger groups. (In chapter 14, some references that detail how to conduct such surveys are listed.) However, a small number of people may provide research information for your writing project without formal research surveys that involve random sampling, sampling error, and all the other trappings of social science research.

How do you decide which people to interview? Ask yourself, Who knows something about this topic? Or, Who do I know who knows somebody knowledgeable about this topic? Most often writers start with the latter question, going to someone who can refer them to someone else.

Once you have names, don't rush out and talk with the people; several important steps come first. Before making any contacts, read several books about your topic to learn its language. During your reading, jot down questions the books do not answer. Second, try to find out as much as you can about the people you will interview— their experiences with the topic, their knowledge of it, and so on. Only then are you ready to contact people and set dates for interviews.

To set up an interview, call the person and make an appointment. Then follow up with a letter. You may want to include in your letter a list of questions you plan to ask so the person has a chance to do some thinking, and perhaps some checking, before you meet with him or her.

Before the interview decide whether you're going to take notes, use a tape recorder, or try to remember everything that is said. I know a few people who neither take notes nor use a tape recorder during an interview. But that procedure takes considerable training and experience, and I wouldn't recommend it. So it's note-taking, a tape recorder, or both. You can use a tape recorder and also take notes, jotting down such observations as the physical surroundings, a description of the person you're interviewing, and anything else that the tape recorder can't capture.

Once at the interview, ask the person if she or he minds whether you tape-record. If there is any reluctance, say, "I want to make sure I quote you accurately." In all the interviewing I've done, I have never been refused. But you may be. It's not all that uncommon. So you must be prepared to take notes just in case. Also, if you're interviewing a person on a controversial topic, state that you will turn off the recorder any time he or she wants to tell you something "off the record." The ethics of interviewing demand that you not use anything you are told off the record.

Talk with the person in his or her place of work or any place that is comfortable. Interviewees are more likely to forget about the tape recorder you're carrying if they are comfortable. Begin with a general question that is easily answered to help the person relax. On informal interviews try to memorize the questions you plan to ask but also remain open to questions not on your list.

Interviewing is truly an art. You need to be constantly alert to keep the person on the topic, yet not cut off interesting answers and anecdotes. Do listen for the anecdotes. A great deal can be learned about a subject area and a person from the stories the person tells you. Some cautions:

1.   Don't talk too much. You are not interviewing yourself. Ask a question and then be quiet. Don't try to put words in the person's mouth or rephrase what he or she is saying with your own words. Listen to the person's words. Don't cut the person off because you believe what he or she has to say isn't relevant. You may find some of those words to be relevant later when you listen to the tape or think about the interview.

2.   Keep the interviewee on the subject. That sounds like a contradiction of number 1, but there are times when an interviewee will wander completely off the subject and begin talking to you about some lawsuit he's involved in or some antique she's recently collected.

3.   Don't let the interviewee become the interviewer. Often the interviewee is interested in your research and begins asking you questions. Some response is necessary, but watch out. You may find when you get home and listen to your tape that the person has interviewed you.

4.   Be flexible with timing. Tell the person before the interview how long it will take so he or she can plan for it. However, plan your own time to accommodate a longer interview because occasionally you will discover a person wants to talk longer and is giving you excellent information.

5.   Payment for an interview? I have never paid anyone for an interview. I have never had anyone suggest payment.

6.   Don't allow the interviewee to censor what you have written. What if the person you interview asks to see what you've written before you submit it for publication or put it in your term paper or report? You may want to send excerpts from what you've written to be sure the facts are correct. But avoid sending the entire article or report. You'll find yourself in a very difficult situation if the person crosses out phrases you like, descriptive material about himself or herself, and so on. If you have a question about a fact, call the person and ask about it.

After the interview is completed, try to transcribe your tape recording and rewrite your notes as soon as possible. One problem with using a tape recorder is the tedious job of transcribing the tape. A recorder that has a foot pedal speeds the operation. A transcription machine, found in most offices, makes it even easier.

Try to get on paper as much information as you can about the setting of the interview and the nonverbal communication that took place. How did the person hold his hands? How did she react to certain questions? Did he smoke during the interview? Did she wear glasses and take them off and put them on? This information will give you something of the context of the situation.

Tape Recorder Tips

Whenever a mechanical device is involved, things can go wrong and often do. But you'll have fewer problems if you follow a few basic guidelines. The tape recorder is an invaluable device when interviewing someone. But it has to work right, or you'll only frustrate yourself and perhaps lose some valuable information.

1.   Understand your recorder. Most failures are not the fault of the recorder but the fault of the operator. Knowing how to put the tape into the machine, knowing which buttons to push for "record," knowing whether the machine warns you when it has run out of tape—all are obvious, yet they often cause problems.

2.   Check the battery charge level if the recorder is battery operated. Most small recorders are battery operated with either regular or rechargeable batteries. If you're going to use regular batteries for an important interview, use new ones to make sure they'll work through the entire interview. If you're going to use rechargeable batteries, recharge them.

3.   Remember that the tape has only two sides. If you're using a tape with thirty minutes of recording time on each side and your interview takes longer than an hour, you may unwittingly turn the tape over again at the end of the second half hour and erase what you recorded during the first half hour. That's easy to do in the excitement of an interview.

4.   Use a remote microphone when you can. Most small cassette recorders have built-in mikes. The problem with built-in mikes is that they pick up all other sounds in the room, including the sound of their own motors. A remote mike, which plugs into the recorder and can be clipped onto the interviewee's clothing, obtains a much higher quality recording than a built-in mike. When recording outdoors, leave the recorder inside a shoulder bag and clip the mike onto the shoulder strap. That will allow the mike to pick up your voice and the voice of the person who is walking with you with little difficulty.

Interviews by Telephone or Letter

The face-to-face interview is the best method to follow when you want information from a relatively small number of people. It supplies background information about them—their office situations, personal mannerisms, and so on.

When people are not readily available, a telephone call or letter is second best. If you know of an expert on your topic who lives 2,000 miles away, a telephone interview can provide some useful information if done properly. Some telephone interview principles:

1. Call and establish a time when you will call again to do the interview. Establish how long the interview will take.

2. Between the first call and the interview, develop a set of questions you want to ask and send them to the person; or when you set the time for the interview, mention the questions you want to cover.

3. Decide whether you want to record your phone conversation. A simple device attached to your recorder and to the telephone allows you to record the message, but you are ethically obligated to have the person's permission to tape, just as in a face-to-face interview. To protect yourself, ask for the person's permission to tape while the recorder is running so his or her voice is on the tape.

4. Have your interview well planned so you can move from question to question but still encourage and allow time for the person to share anecdotes.

If you want to contact more people than you can reasonably expect to call on the telephone in a short period of time, interview them through the mail. Some principles to follow when using the mail:

1. Send a personal letter to each person and enclose a self-addressed, stamped envelope for the reply.

2. Make your letter short and your questions specific. Don't do as a student did a few years ago when he wrote and asked, "Could you tell me about writing?" Keep the number of questions to a minimum. The longer the list of questions, the more likely the letter will be tossed.

Observation

Still another source of information is what you observe. Anthropologists and scientists have used this approach for years as they set up experiments and then observed results. Yet it's possible to obtain much valuable information without setting up experiments if you train yourself to be an observer. Because of the thousands of stimuli you encounter every day, you have learned to "tune out" much of what is going on around you. You must learn to selectively observe situations if you are to obtain accurate and complete information. Some guidelines for observing:

1.   Try to avoid placing everything and everyone you observe immediately into some type of category. Try to observe unencumbered by categories; they can come later. By placing everything immediately into a category, you may short-circuit what you're observing and not see it completely.

2.   Be aware of distorted perceptions. Your background and experience affect what you observe and how you observe it. The very angle that you use to look at something affects what you see. Let's say you look at a closed door and are asked to describe it. You observe that the door is approximately 7 feet tall and perhaps 3½ feet wide. But open the door so you can see only the edge of it and then describe what you see. Now it's perhaps only 3 inches wide. It's the same door but viewed from two different perspectives. The same is true of other observations of people, places, things, moods, and feelings.

3.   Know that your emotional state will influence what you observe. If you observe a political demonstration and it makes you angry, your anger will influence your observations and color what you write. One way to counter this problem is to write your observations immediately following the event and then evaluate what you've written sometime later.

4.   Be a cautious participant. Sometimes it's necessary to join an organization or become a participant in a group to observe it. You must balance the extent to which you are an observer and the extent to which you are a participant. The more you participate, the more likely it is that you will lose your detached observer's view. The participant-observer technique has become popular with many professional writers these days. One case in point is Gay Talese's book *Thy Neighbor's Wife,* for which Talese participated in many of the activities he wrote about.

5.   Examine other evidence. To avoid some distorted perceptions, seek other evidence. Compare what you observe with what others have observed, or read reports about the situation you are observing.

The Process of Researching

It's possible to find facts in many places: previous experience, a clipping file, the library, people, and observation. Which approach should you use? How should you plan your research time? These are important questions but difficult ones to answer.

The approach to use depends on what you're trying to find out. If you're working on a market research project, you could look at customer sales records, read books on market research, interview top sales representatives, and perhaps interview some customers. To research whether your company should buy a new piece of equipment, you could read literature from the equipment suppliers, talk with sales representatives, analyze costs, interview present equipment operators, visit another plant where the new equipment is being used, and so on.

As you already know, you must plan your research by thinking of questions before you go to the library, organizing your interview before you meet with the person, and thinking carefully before you phone or write someone for information. But you should not be so organized that you miss what I call the serendipity of researching—being open to surprise. What you haven't planned can be the most valuable.

When you're reading, you'll discover angles to your research that you hadn't thought about. Sometimes these new angles will cause you to rethink the project you're working on. At times, when you're beginning to research a project, you don't know enough about the project to ask questions. Researching is a way to learn about the project so you can plan the rest of what you do. So although a research project should be guided, you should be open to new directions and new information as you discover them.

Are Your Facts Accurate?

Anyone who has ever done research knows how difficult it is to be accurate, yet you are obligated to be as accurate as possible. That takes some special attention and often additional work. Some principles to follow to help ensure greater accuracy in research:

1. Develop a skeptical attitude. Never accept anything at face value, particularly if it sounds as if it couldn't possibly be false. Learn to question, to doubt, to wonder if there are other possibilities.

2.   Be aware of your own biases. Be especially skeptical of those ideas and people who agree with you and what you believe. In cases where what someone says is what you believe, search for the opposite opinion. A good principle to follow is this: You can't know what you believe until you know what you don't believe.

3.   Try to find more than one perspective. If you're observing something, try to see it from different time perspectives, different space perspectives, different distance perspectives. How does it look up close? How does it look at a distance? How does it look in the morning? in the late afternoon?

Searching for more than one perspective applies to abstract ideas too. Let's say you're writing a paper about behavior modification. When you read reports written by those supporting a behaviorist position, you gain one perspective on the values and approaches to behavior modification. But if you seek out some who call themselves humanistic psychologists, you discover quite another perspective. The two opposing perspectives help you see your topic more broadly and completely.

Searching for more than one perspective not only helps you find a more complete picture of an idea or situation, but it also helps you discover the truth. Let's say you interview two people about an event and they contradict each other about what they saw. They may be reporting their perceptions accurately, but we are all prone to error in what we see. By going to a third person, perhaps to a fourth and a fifth, you can come closer to learning the truth of the situation.

4.   Use original sources when you can. If you are interviewing a person and she begins telling what a friend believes about something, you'd better interview the friend. If you are researching an idea from history and the history book you're reading reports on ideas from a journal, you'll want to read the journal yourself. Of course, this assumes that the idea is of sufficient importance to your project to take the time for inspecting the original documents. By taking research material from secondary sources, you run the risk of compounding mistakes the first researcher made—mistakes in spelling, mistakes in dates, mistakes in interpretations of ideas. Many mistakes are made in the process of reporting on material taken from original sources.

5.   Try to establish the credibility of your sources. What background and experience do they have? What makes them knowledgeable about the topic? Who published the book you're using as a reference? Did the author publish it himself? If you're interviewing a middle-management business person and she has recently been fired from her job, this may have a great effect on what she says.

If you can find out something about the organizations to which a person belongs, you can often understand better why he or she is saying something and establish the credibility of the comments.

6. Be cautious about sampling. You obviously don't need to talk with every secretary in a typing pool to understand opinions about microcomputers and word processors. But which ones *do* you talk to? I'm reminded of the old story about the person eating soup that was too salty. One teaspoon of soup and the person knew the answer; the entire bowl need not be tasted. But what if the question was, What are the vegetables in the bowl of soup? If the first teaspoon brought up a carrot among the beans, the person would report carrots and beans. But that spoonful may have missed the corn that was also in the bowl.

Try to get a representative sample. That means talk to secretaries who are relatively new on the job as well as those who have been there for several years. Talk to those who wear glasses as well as those who do not (some complaints about computers involve eyestrain). Try to think of the variations among the secretaries that may affect their responses to your questions about computers.

In chapter 14 some reference books on research that include procedures for sampling, including how to do a scientific random sample, are listed.

EXERCISES

1. Select a question and go to the library to research the answer. Record what happens in your Writing Log.
2. Use a personal experience as a research source in your Writing Log.
3. Record any other "research" experiences you've had recently— interviews, observations, readings. What problems and frustrations did you encounter? How did you overcome them?
4. Start a personal journal in which you record day-to-day activities and your reactions to them. This will give you a record of experiences and feelings that could be used as examples for some writing projects.

Chapter 4

Discovering Your Own
Approach to Writing

If your readers tell you your writing is dull, if you have trouble writing what you mean, if writing is unsatisfying, the trouble may be in your approach. What approach do you follow when you have something to write?

Some people assume approach means style—the way you string words together to create tone and meaning. Style *is* part of approach, but an approach to writing is much more. Approach includes how you generate ideas, how you organize your thoughts, how you put your thoughts on paper, how you go about solving a particular writing problem. Approach is how you develop the beginning and the end for a piece of writing and everything in between.

Approaches to writing are extremely individual, no matter what some writing instructors say. No one writing approach fits all people and all writing situations. You need to work out for yourself an approach or approaches that feel right for you and accomplish your purpose for writing.

The following factors will influence your writing approach:

• Your audience. Are you writing for colleagues in your organization, for a professor in a class you are taking, or for a national audience of professionals? Your audience will make a difference in how you put your words together.

• Your purpose for writing. Are you trying to describe, narrate, explain, criticize, or persuade? (See chapter 6 for specific information about these purposes for writing.)

• What you are writing. Are you writing a report, a newsletter, an article for publication, a book review, a memo, or a thesis? Your approach will vary from genre to genre. How much time do you have for the writing project? How much research is involved? How long will the completed project be? Often the overall writing project will dictate the writing approach you use. A one-page memo to an employee may involve many hours of time but take quite a different approach from that of a thirty-page term paper.

• The subject of your writing. Certain subjects go well with certain approaches. For example, if you are reporting on the operation of a new office machine and why your firm should consider purchasing it, a straight-line writing approach is likely most applicable. If, however, you are describing a marketing approach for a new product, a developmental writing approach may be more useful.

• What works well for you. The approach to writing that works well for you, though influenced by the above factors, is extremely important in finally deciding the writing approach you will follow.

Two General Approaches to Writing

Two approaches followed by many writers these days, whether they are aware of it or not, are the straight-line approach and the developmental approach.

The Straight-Line Approach

You are already familiar with the straight-line approach to writing. It is the one taught in many English departments and journalism fea-ture-writing courses. The straight-line approach includes the following steps: (1) selecting a topic, (2) doing the research, (3) writing an outline, (4) writing a rough draft, and (5) revising and rewriting the rough draft.

The Process of Straight-Line Writing

1. Select a topic. As simple as that sounds, selecting a topic is often a difficult task. No matter what the situation, most writers make the mistake of selecting a topic that is too broad.

Sometimes it's necessary to begin research on a topic to discover how broad it really is. For example, if you are writing about leadership styles for the company newsletter, you may discover, once you research your topic, that it is far too broad. You will then need to narrow it down, perhaps to recent research on leadership styles.

It often helps to state your topic in question form. Questions to be answered are excellent guides to research.

2.   Do the research. Refer to chapter 3 for information about researching and research approaches.

3.   Write an outline (an idea guide). To those who suffered through high school English courses in which formal outlining was taught, that may sound like an ominous suggestion. But an outline need not be formal. When outlining, go through all your research notes and list all the ideas you have. Then organize those ideas into different combinations, thinking through the relationship of the ideas to one another and to the overall piece of writing. Figure out an overall structure for the writing by deciding whether you should organize the material around major ideas with subideas under each; around chronological time (first this happened, and then this happened); around space (this happened in this part of the country, and that happened in another part); going from the simple to the complex; and so on. Usually the topic and the research suggest the best organization for a piece of writing (see chapter 5). The purpose for your writing (see chapter 6) will also influence how you organize your ideas.

4.   Write a rough draft. With the outline, or idea guide, alongside your typewriter and your research notes handy, begin writing. Be careful, though, that you don't become a slave to the outline. During the process of writing, you may discover a new way of organizing your ideas. Remember, the outline is a guide, not a prescription. Write the entire piece, whether it's a section for your thesis or a newsletter, before you begin revising and rewriting. Stopping to correct spelling errors or to change clumsy sentences usually stops the flow of creative juices. Write the entire piece and then set it aside for at least a day before you begin revising it.

5.   Revise and rewrite. After the writing has cooled, begin revising. Not to wait for the writing to cool is a mistake because in the heat of writing you'll see little fault in what you've produced. After it has cooled for a time, you can usually spot many errors. (Chapter 9 discusses revising and rewriting in depth.)

Advantages and Disadvantages

One advantage of the straight-line approach to writing is that it emphasizes clear thinking before the writer begins to commit words to paper, saving a great deal of time and effort. Usually less revision is needed because the major work has been done in arranging and rearranging the ideas.

Also, most writing situations lend themselves to a straight-line approach. We describe something to someone, we explain, we criticize, or we persuade. Most people in our society have been trained to think in a straight-line fashion, considering questions and problems in an orderly way. The straight-line approach is an orderly process.

On the other hand, the straight-line approach, particularly in its more pure forms, has disadvantages as well. Straight-line writing is often criticized for being mechanical and uncreative. Thus, it can be boring and unimaginative to the reader. It tends to draw on the objective, analytic side of the brain, often at the expense of the subjective, intuitive side. Thus, linear writing is often cold and without feeling.

Straight-line writing is often unsatisfying to the writer. It can become just another mechanical task, not too different from the many other mechanical tasks a writer faces. And it denies the times when you can't think through what you have to say until you begin writing. Some ideas are developed, not in a straight-line way, but in a developmental way as you work at successive views of an idea. The idea develops only as you write, think, research, and then write, think, and research some more. Straight-line writing denies that some ideas start with the germ and then move in a spiral, expanding the ideas from a variety of perspectives that come into focus during the process of writing.

The Developmental Approach

Rather than a straight-line movement from idea to completed manuscript, developmental writing assumes a series of activities that move back and forth, often in a spiral fashion, until a manuscript is completed. Developmental writing assumes that not all writers can think through what they have to say before they begin writing.

You will discover, if you haven't already, that there are times when no matter how much thinking and research you have done on a writing project, you still don't know what to write. You will also discover that by writing whatever comes to you, you begin to make sense out of the project. The process of writing gets the creative

juices flowing and triggers the thinking process, and these two human processes begin to interact with and enrich each other. You
write and you think, and you think and you write, and the processes
become intertwined. You rewrite and you think, and you think and
you rewrite, until the ideas become sharper and more complete.

Peter Elbow[1] suggests abandoning linear writing in favor of developmental writing. He suggests that when you face a writing assignment—a term paper, the first section of your dissertation, a company
report, a newsletter, or a memo—you sit down and begin writing.

The Process of Developmental Writing

1. Write whatever comes into your mind, but keep writing. Put
all your ideas down as quickly as you can. Write without worrying
about sentence structure, grammar, or misspelled words.
Concentrate on putting what is in your head on paper.

2. Once you've finished the first draft, begin reading and
reorganizing what you wrote. Look for the organization of ideas, the
omission of ideas, and whether the theme is coming through as
you intended.

3. Write another draft, starting with the corrections and
additions needed.

4. Revise again, once more looking for the big ideas and
whether they have been communicated. Also look for the flow of
the piece and for any slow, vague, and unexciting sections of your
writing.

5. Write still another draft.

6. Revise once more; this time pay particular attention to
spelling, grammar, and the other details of good writing.

7. Write a final draft, taking into account the fine tuning you
did during the last revision.

Advantages and Disadvantages

Developmental writing frees you from becoming a slave to your
research and the notes you have taken. Prior to writing the piece, you
may have done considerable reading and taken many notes. But with
a developmental approach, you write the first draft with your notes
set aside. It therefore helps you put *you* into your writing. It helps you
find out exactly what you have to say on a subject and not just repeat
what others have said.

The developmental approach calls on the side of the brain that
considers the unconscious and creative elements of life, the side that

puts ideas together in new and unusual ways. Developmental writing is tied to such brain activities because it is less structured and pre-planned, thus allowing new ideas to emerge during the process of writing. And these new ideas are expressed in new and interesting ways that you hadn't thought about prior to beginning to write.

Once you've practiced a bit, you'll find that developmental writing flows easily. The words begin to pour out as fast as you are able to put them down. Also, it focuses on the overall message and the overall tone or feeling of a piece of writing. If you write with the entire piece in mind, you don't get bogged down with individual sections.

For many people, developmental writing is fun, even for those who don't usually enjoy writing. A kind of release comes when a person can just sit down and write, without worrying whether the sentences are just right or the words are spelled correctly. The straight-line approach to writing puts much more emphasis on getting it right the first time, on writing as best you can so little time is spent revising. In the process, many people are so concerned that their first draft will not be of high quality that they don't write at all.

But developmental writing has problems too. It usually results in discarding much material. Words, paragraphs, often entire pages of writing are tossed because they are repetitious or irrelevant to the main focus of the work. Sometimes developmental writing dredges up unconscious ideas and words that seem meaningful at the moment but later make no sense whatsoever. Some people even argue that developmental writing does not lead to clear thinking but simply records the muddled thinking of a person who can't figure out what to say.

Developmental writing, though producing many words in a short time, ultimately takes much time because several drafts and considerable editing, revising, and rewriting are required.

Those who are highly structured and have many years of experience in thinking and organizing before writing may have considerable difficulty switching to a developmental approach to writing. It assumes a richness of the unconscious mind, which is tapped during the developmental writing process. Not everyone may be able to find such richness.

Which Approach to Follow

Which approach should you follow, the straight-line approach or the developmental approach? One way to make such a decision is to look at the kind of person and writer you are.

If you are a highly organized person who does research, thinks through carefully every idea, keeps extensive notes and organizes them well before beginning to write, you may find an occasional attempt at developmental writing useful. Or if you are a free spirit who finds thinking and organizing difficult without writing first, consider trying a straight-line approach now and then.

It's also possible to combine the two approaches. Let's say you are primarily a straight-line writer and you have a topic to write about. You might consider following a developmental approach before you begin researching the topic. This may be impossible for some topics, but for others, you may be surprised. You may remember experiences you've had related to the topic that you hadn't thought of before; you may also discover new perspectives on the questions. All of this could come out during the first draft attempt. You will also likely discover the major holes in your presentation, the questions that remain to be answered. So the first writing attempt can also have an assessment function for you. Once you've completed your research, you might return to developmental writing before you work on an outline. This could result in putting the research together in new ways.

On the other hand, if you are primarily a developmental writer now, you might find it useful to incorporate some of the straight-line writing approaches into your writing. You might do this by researching a topic in some depth before you begin writing so you will have a strong sense of what the topic is about. You may find it helpful, after you write the first draft with a developmental approach, to work out a brief outline of what you've said in the first draft and add to the outline when necessary before beginning the second draft.

By combining the two approaches to writing and emphasizing the approach that you don't ordinarily follow, you take advantage of some of the good features of both approaches while eliminating some of the problems with each. Unfortunately, the tendency is to follow one approach or the other without attempting to combine them. Some writing teachers advise following the developmental approach only. Others never offer an alternative to the straight-line approach, not even recognizing there is another approach to writing.

If you are a writer who doesn't have an approach, I encourage you to incorporate some of both the straight-line approach and the developmental approach in your own writing. So much writing these days, especially that written by students, does not include much of the writer in the writing. Following some of the developmental approach ensures that your writing has both you and your meaning about a topic deeply incorporated into the piece. In addition, your writing will be more interesting to you and to your readers.

Our Two-Sided Brain

Understanding something about how our brains work helps us understand the difference between straight-line and developmental writing and particularly what happens when we try to combine the two approaches.

Brain researchers tell us that our brains have two sides; each side makes different contributions to our thinking and our performance. The left side of the brain is logical, analytical, and verbal. It considers ideas that are precise. It is most comfortable moving step by step to solve problems and reach decisions. It is also judgmental.

The right side of the brain considers feelings and emotions rather than concrete facts and is intuitive and nonlinear in thinking. It operates in our subconscious or preconscious, so we often aren't even aware that it is operating at all. It relies on nonverbal imagery. It is nonjudgmental and willing to suspend opinion.

All of us have experienced both-side brain activities. However, some have suppressed the right side of the brain so often for certain tasks that it has all but ceased functioning. The scientific method relies heavily on the left side of the brain. Problem solving, in which you systematically define a problem, search for solutions, select a solution, and test it, relies on left-side brain operations. Many of us have been taught to be precise with numbers—computers force us to be these days—and to make yes or no decisions about many of the questions and problems we face in life. These operations rest in the left side of the brain.

On the other hand, creative people such as artists, novelists, poets, musicians, and dancers rely on the right side of their brain for much of their creative activity.

Most of us approach writing as a left-side brain operation. As a result, much of our writing is cold and lifeless, lacking feeling and the spark of creativity that could set it apart from the thousands of lines of boring, uninspired writing we must read every day.

John Hersey[2] calls the right side of the brain the *supplier* for the writer and the left side the *censor*. He says writers need to cultivate the activity of both sides of the brain. The supplier has access to our primary feelings. It acts in an uninhibited, unknowing way—we are not aware of what it does. As a result, the supplier plays with our ideas when we aren't aware of what it is doing, putting them together in a variety of ways that may seem totally unrealistic to us when we become conscious of them (sometimes they *are* totally unrealistic). The supplier considers the writing project we are working on as a whole in ways that are new and different—*if* we give it the opportunity to do so.

You have experienced the operation of the right side of your brain many times in your life. Sometimes it is called insight. At one time or another, you most likely have had a problem that you tried to solve and worked at solving until you gave up. You went off to do something else, only to have the answer to the problem flash into your head as if from nowhere. The right side of your brain was working on the solution all the while, and when you least suspected, you became conscious of it.

People often are aware of their right-side brain operation just before they go to sleep. Others wake up in the middle of the night with insightful ideas. Still others are in touch with the operation of the right side of their brains when they are jogging or during other repetitive physical exercise. Some find their right-side brain operation is enhanced when they are relaxing.

In calling the left side of the brain the censor, Hersey means it selects and organizes from the supplier. It interprets and makes sense out of what the supplier offers. The censor is necessary for the writer to keep the supplier from running amok. Unfortunately, most people have such inhibited suppliers that the censors have taken over the writing function.

The supplier has its problems when working alone. Without the censor, the supplier provides a disjointed, often unending flurry of words that are unorganized and illogical. On the other hand, the censor has the nasty habit of being overly judgmental, wanting to throw out new ideas offered by the supplier before they are given any attention at all.

Ideally, then, for the writer, a healthy tension should exist between the right and left sides of the brain. The right side should be cultivated to provide new ideas, new combinations of ideas, and new ways of expressing old ideas. The left side should be called on to organize and make sense out of the creations of the right side. Both sides are essential.

Because many of us have suppressed the right side of our brains for so long when writing, it may be necessary to help your supplier become an equal partner. Following are exercises for encouraging right-side brain activity.

Right-Side Brain Exercises

1. Think of the times when you've had insights or creative thoughts. Write them down. Then think about what you were doing when you got each insight. Were you running, drifting into sleep, daydreaming, fishing, playing golf, chopping wood, working in your garden, hiking a quiet trail? When you are faced with a writing problem, when you have something to say but don't quite know how to say it, return to that particular activity and see whether another insight will come. Unfortunately, the very nature of right-side brain activity is unpredictable, so you can't *make* it work for you. But you can work at providing the conditions under which it has worked before.

2. Think about a time when you had a creative experience (it doesn't have to be a writing experience). Perhaps you were working on your car, and you solved a problem in a new way. Or perhaps you designed and sewed a piece of clothing you were particularly proud of. With a little thought, you should be able to come up with several of these experiences. Once you have identified several, jot them down on a piece of paper. Then think about the one you remember most vividly, particularly in terms of your satisfaction with the project. Focus on how you felt at the time. Try to remember the feeling as vividly as you can, recalling every detail of what you did and how you felt about it. When you are faced with a situation demanding a creative solution, think back to the example and the feelings you had at the time. Recalling the situation and feelings may be enough to start the creative juices of the right side of the brain operating again.

3. Do physical exercise of a repetitive nature. Many people who jog or walk regularly find these to be creative times.

4. Do a relaxation exercise. Sit quietly in a chair with your eyes closed and think about each part of your anatomy, starting with your toes. Think about the space within your toes, then move to your feet, and so on until you are thinking about the space within your head. Think about all the space within you. Open your eyes and begin writing.

5. Another relaxation exercise is to first tense and then relax each of your body parts in turn. Start with your toes, tensing them and relaxing them, then move to your feet, then your ankles, and so on until you are tensing and relaxing the muscles in your face and head. Begin writing.

6. Set a timer for five minutes. Sit quietly and imagine yourself outside of your body and observing your thoughts. When you find yourself being critical, take a deep breath. When the time is up, write down as quickly as you can your impressions of your thoughts.

7. Do free writing. Set a timer for ten minutes. Begin writing and keep writing until the timer rings. If you can't think of anything to write, write, "I can't think of anything to write." If you think the idea isn't a particularly good one, write, "I think this is a dumb idea." But keep writing until the ten minutes are up. Do this several days in a row, perhaps increasing the time to fifteen minutes or even half an hour. You will be surprised at what will appear on your paper.

8. Put the right side of your brain in conscious opposition to the left side. To do this, list several of the ideas you are writing about. Have the left side of your brain criticize each idea in turn, ruthlessly stating what is wrong with it. Describe in detail the complaint. Then have the left side ask the right side to offer something better, taking into account the complaints.

Now switch to the right side. Offer as many suggestions as you can to change and improve upon the idea without allowing yourself to be interrupted by the left side of the brain and its critical comments. Once more switch to the left side and evaluate the several suggestions the right side has offered.

Reflect on the entire process. Have you added to the ideas you originally listed? Have you gotten any new insights?

9. Devise your own system for getting in touch with your unconscious. You may want to combine several of the above or come up with some of your own.

Writer's Block

Go to any writers' workshop, talk to any professional writer, in fact, talk to anyone with responsibility for writing, and one of the topics that comes up often is writer's block. Writer's block is when you can't write. You know you must. You have the information. You have a deadline, and yet you can't think of a thing to say. You sit staring at the typewriter keys, or perhaps you clean the machine or arrange the paper in a creative way. If you write with a pen, you may fool with the paper or doodle in the corners. But no words appear on the paper, and you declare that you have writer's block.

For some people, writer's block is like mid-life crisis. You really haven't arrived until you have had it. Writer's block is a fashionable thing for some people. It's also very troublesome, for nothing gets done when you're going through it. I have seen graduate students who are writing dissertations develop writer's block. They completed many graduate courses, worked hard collecting data for their research projects, and then, just when they are on the verge of receiving their Ph.D. degrees, they are unable to write their dissertations.

What Causes Writer's Block?

The single most pervasive reason for writer's block is trying to write a final draft the first time. You write a sentence or two, perhaps even a couple of pages, and then read through it and decide you aren't ready to write because the writing is so rough.

Procrastination is another reason. And it relates to discipline. A writer, whether he or she is writing a memo or a 300-page book manuscript, must sit down and do it. For most of us, there are a hundred reasons that we shouldn't write right now but later. Perhaps we think we will feel more creative at another time, or our heads will be clearer, or the house will be quieter, or the office will be in less turmoil. So we put it off, and it doesn't get done. Then we face a deadline and are forced to write quickly. It isn't our best effort because we haven't put in enough time, and we get further reinforcement for the notion that we really can't write very well anyway.

The best way to overcome writer's block is to prevent it from happening. Here are some techniques.

1. If you are working on a report that you know will be about thirty pages long, make a goal that you will do five pages a day until the report is finished. No matter what happens, make sure that five pages are completed each day.

2. To ensure that you meet your goal, select a time in the day for your writing. It might be the first thing you do early in the morning, or it could be late at night. The time doesn't matter. What does matter for many writers is having a specific time each day for writing.

3. When writing, don't look back to correct spelling errors, clumsy sentences, and punctuation. Keep on going until the first draft is finished.

4. Select a place for writing that has a minimum of distractions. The phone won't ring to interrupt you, someone won't stop by to see you, or external noises aren't so excessive that you can't concentrate on what you are doing.

5.   Give yourself a reward when you've finished your assigned quota. The reward might be a second cup of coffee or time to read a favorite book.

6.   Buy a notebook and keep a record of the pages you write each day. In that way, you can see your progress. This is particularly helpful if you are writing a longer piece, say a thesis or dissertation for which you know you must eventually create 200 or more pages.

But let's say you've tried these techniques and you're still blocked. The thesis or report deadline is approaching, and you can't get started. You can't think of anything to say. You've got all the information you need, but nothing happens. What can you do?

1.   Find someone who will listen, and talk to him or her about your project. Often the creative juices will flow as soon as the words begin to form. Speaking the words is easier than writing them.

2.   Talk your paper, your thesis, or whatever writing project is giving you problems into a tape recorder. I'm not suggesting you dictate it, though you might want to try that to get you started. (For most people, dictating results in far too many words.)

3.   If you have already written some of the report, retype the last page. Often that will be enough to get you started again.

4.   Try free writing. Time yourself for ten minutes, and write about your topic without stopping. Don't worry about how the ideas go together or even whether what you are writing makes any sense. Just write as rapidly as you can for ten minutes.

5.   Write a letter to a friend. Putting ideas into words on a topic quite different from that of your writing project may be enough to get you started.

6.   Exercise. Jog or walk around the block. Chop wood. Do twenty situps. Work up a sweat, take a hot shower, and try again. Sometimes being away from the writing for a time is the very thing that gets you started again.

7.   Try writing in longhand if you ordinarily use a typewriter. Or if you ordinarily write in longhand and know how to type, try using the typewriter. The break in approach may be enough to start you going again.

8.   If the beginning of a piece gives you the most problems— and beginnings *do* bother many writers—work your way through your beginning by telling yourself that you probably won't use the beginning you have written anyway (you probably won't). Force yourself to keep writing past the beginning rather than tearing sheet after sheet out of your typewriter because you weren't satisfied with the first paragraph.

9. Try one of the relaxation exercises mentioned in the previous section.

EXERCISES

1. In your Writer's Log, note the writing approach that you follow most often. Describe it. Is it more straight line or developmental?
2. Record your reactions to the right-side brain exercises you tried. To what extent did they work? Did they cause you to feel any differently about your writing? Have you seen any changes in what you have written after completing the exercises?
3. If you have experienced writer's block, note why you believe it occurred. How did you overcome it?

NOTES

1. Peter Elbow, *Writing Without Teachers* (New York: Oxford University Press, 1973).
2. John Hersey, ed., *The Writer's Craft* (New York: Alfred A. Knopf, 1974).

Chapter 5

Beginnings, Middles, and Endings

No matter what writing approach you use, you must consider carefully how you begin, how you end, and obviously what you put in between. These three fundamental parts of every piece of writing present problems to many writers. When they're not done well, the readers suffer too.

Writing the Lead

Let's start with the beginning, or the "lead" (the term journalists use). The lead is the first few sentences of a news story. In longer pieces, it is as long as the first few paragraphs. The lead does three things: it captures the reader's attention, provides the reader an idea of what to expect, and compels the reader to go on. If your lead is poorly done, you're apt to lose your reader in the first few seconds, and your entire piece of writing may be lost, no matter how brilliant the rest of the piece happens to be.

If you're a student, you're probably smiling at this point. Why worry about a lead, you ask, when you know your professor *has* to read what you write? Professors, too, appreciate good writing. A term paper or research report that begins with a well-written lead captures the professor's attention. And though he or she may have to read your entire piece, the chances of a favorable reaction (better grade) are greater if you've written a compelling lead.

If you are responsible for writing your organization's newsletter, or if you write memos or proposals, you may wonder why no one reads them as often or as carefully as you believe they should. Perhaps your leads stop the reading process before it ever starts.

Leads may be written in several ways. You could ask your readers a question or questions. For example, a lead I once wrote was this:

> Why do we have problems understanding human beings? Why do we spend time considering this question when other seemingly more important problems beg for attention?
> Certainly our understanding of human beings and particularly human adults is crucial to everything we do as educators of adults. As educators, we enter the lives of other people.[1]

You could use a narrative lead that describes some incident or anecdote. For instance, in *Cosmos* Carl Sagan began a chapter thus:

> Many years ago, so the story goes, a celebrated newspaper publisher sent a telegram to a noted astronomer: WIRE COLLECT IMMEDIATELY FIVE HUNDRED WORDS ON WHETHER THERE IS LIFE ON MARS. The astronomer dutifully replied: NOBODY KNOWS, NOBODY KNOWS, NOBODY KNOWS . . . 250 times.[2]

Alvin Toffler wrote this lead for a chapter in *Future Shock* introducing the idea of the temporariness of modern life:

> Each spring an immense lemming-like migration begins all over the Eastern United States. Singly and in groups, burdened with sleeping bags, blankets and bathing suits, some 15,000 American college students toss aside their texts and follow a highly accurate homing instinct that leads them to the sun-bleached shoreline of Fort Lauderdale, Florida.[3]

Another kind of lead is an unusual statement, something that will capture the reader's attention *because* it is unusual. For instance, in the first chapter of *Future Shock,* Toffler begins with this:

> In the three short decades between now and the twenty-first century, millions of ordinary, psychologically normal people will face an abrupt collision with the future.[4]

Still another approach is to begin with a quotation. The quotation may be from someone you've interviewed for your writing assignment, or it may be a quotation you've read someplace (be careful about permissions for published pieces, especially if you are quoting from a poem or a song—see chapter 3). To introduce a chapter about the intelligence of animals, Sagan wrote:

"Beasts abstract not," announced John Locke, expressing mankind's prevailing opinion throughout recorded history. Bishop Berkeley had, however, a sardonic rejoinder: "If the fact that brutes abstract not be made the distinguishing property of that sort of animal, I fear a great many of those that pass for men must be reckoned into their number."[5]

A final approach is to write your lead as journalists do, answering who, what, where, when, and why all in the first few sentences. For instance, a Wisconsin newspaper report started with the following paragraphs:

A Waunakee bush pilot caused police a few problems and Atwood Avenue area residents a few worries Sunday night when he decided to visit some friends and turned Olbrich Park into an impromptu landing strip.
   The plane, a 1939 Stinson single-engine, landed safely after buzzing the park on two passes about 10 feet off the ground.[6]

The particular approach used in writing a lead isn't nearly as important as whether it works. Does it capture the reader's attention and get him or her into the piece of writing?

William Zinsser sums up writing leads this way: "There can be no fixed rules for how to write a lead. Within the broad principle of not letting the reader get away, every writer must approach his subject in a manner that most naturally suits what he is writing about and who he is."[7]

Writing the Ending

Second in importance to the lead is the ending. What kind of impression do you want to leave with your readers when they have finished reading (assuming you've kept their attention to the end)? The ending gives you a chance to tie together what you've said, but you must be careful not to write the piece over again in shortened form.

A summary should leave your reader with a positive impression and perhaps an interest in following up on the topic and reading more of your writing. For longer pieces of writing, say a long report or a monograph, you could include a section at the end entitled "Summary," in which you emphasize the major points of the piece. Sometimes it is appropriate to include the summary at the very beginning of a piece of writing, so the reader has a quick overview. That approach is often followed in proposal writing and in some kinds of reports.

A summary can also be in the form of a question, a quotation, and/or a recommendation (depending on your purpose for writing). For example, Carl Sagan ended a chapter on earth's ability to support life this way:

> Our intelligence and our technology have given us the power to affect the climate. How will we use this power? Are we willing to tolerate ignorance and complacency in matters that affect the entire human family? Do we value short-term advantages above the welfare of the Earth? Or will we think on longer time scales, with concern for our children and our grandchildren, to understand and protect the complex life-support systems of our planet? The Earth is a tiny and fragile world. It needs to be cherished.[8]

When faced with writing a beginning and an ending, forget about them and just start writing. Your lead idea and your ending will come to you when you've put your middle on paper.

Writing the Middle

The middle is where you elaborate the content of your writing. Much of the rest of this book is concerned with what you write between the beginning and the end.

Organizing Material

How should you organize what you write? No matter what approach you use, you must figure out a way in which you will present your material. The way in which you came upon ideas in your research is not necessarily the order in which you should present them. Also, don't assume that the first way you decide to organize your material is necessarily the best way. Be open to changing the organization as you work on the project.

A rule of thumb when organizing material is to ask, What way of presenting the material best makes the point? Purpose for writing, audience, and content all influence the way in which you present your ideas. You can arrange material following (1) chronological order, (2) space sequence, (3) an inductive or a deductive approach, (4) a major topics approach, or (5) some combination of these.

Chronological Order

Chronological order means reporting how something occurred through time. If you're telling someone how to do something, you lay out a series of steps: first you do this, then you do this, and so on. If you're describing something that occurred, it often makes sense to describe it according to the way it happened: first this happened, then this happened, and so on.

Space Sequence

If you're describing the various fixtures in a room, or if you're writing about what happened in different parts of the country, you're using a space sequence. Sometimes it makes sense to combine chronological order and space sequence when you're describing something involving both time and space. For instance, if you're writing a term paper about a Civil War battle, you would likely want to describe the various physical aspects of the battlefield, what events happened, where they happened, and when they happened.

Inductive and Deductive Approaches

When following the inductive approach, you present evidence and then make your point, based on your evidence, at the end of the piece. There can be no conclusion that does not relate directly to the evidence. Let's say you're writing about the employment situation for teenagers in your community. You might write about the various employers and the number of young people they employ each year. You could include information about layoff rates, required job training, salary levels, and so on. And if your point for writing the piece is to show that your community has limited opportunities for young people, you then make such a concluding statement, based, of course, on the evidence you've presented.

When following the deductive approach, you begin with a conclusion or a premise. Then you present an argument to support your premise. The evidence you use is more illustrative than exhaustive. For example, in writing the article about inadequate job opportunities for teenagers, you might begin with a statement such as, "The unemployment rate for the youth of our city is too high." You then proceed to support your point by citing examples: numbers of teenagers hired by various employers, layoff rates, and so on.

Major Topics

Material written to describe or explain is often best arranged following a major topics approach. That is the approach most often used when writing a thesis or dissertation, in which the major topics are a research problem, importance of research, research methods, related research, presentation of data, conclusions, and suggestions for further research.

Of course, the major topics approach may be combined with either the inductive or the deductive approach when you are trying to argue a point and convince someone of something. Major topics, with supporting evidence, can be used to make your argument. Be careful, though. The major topics approach is often the most obvious approach to follow when organizing your writing; it may not be the *best* approach. Explore other approaches, particularly if you believe that the major topics approach is the only way to organize your material.

EXERCISES

1. Find four or five things you have written recently. Select both longer and shorter pieces. They can be reports, memos, assignments for school, etc. Then analyze each one by answering these questions:

   What kind of lead did you use? How effective is the lead based on the points made at the beginning of the chapter? Did the lead capture the reader's attention? Did it tell the reader what to expect? Did it compel the reader to go on?

   What kind of ending did you write? How effective was it in your judgment? Did it present a concluding thought or suggest an action?

   How did you organize your ideas? What alternative organization could you have followed?

2. In your Writing Log, note problems you've had in writing leads and endings or in organizing material. After trying some of the suggestions in this chapter, note how well they worked for you.

NOTES

1. Jerold W. Apps, *Problems in Continuing Education* (New York: McGraw-Hill, 1979), p. 27.
2. Carl Sagan, *Cosmos* (New York: Random House, 1980), p. 106.

3. Alvin Toffler, *Future Shock* (New York: Random House, 1970), p. 83.
4. Ibid., p. 9.
5. Carl Sagan, *The Dragons of Eden* (New York: Random House, 1977), p. 107.
6. *Wisconsin State Journal,* July 3, 1972.
7. William Zinsser, *On Writing Well,* 2nd ed. (New York: Harper & Row, 1980), p. 69.
8. Sagan, *Cosmos,* p. 103.

Chapter 6

Writing for Different Purposes

Deciding why you're writing something is the crucial starting point. Sometimes the form of writing—a business letter that tells someone he or she has been turned down for a job, a term paper that discusses an environmental issue, a report about a piece of research—helps clarify the purpose of your writing. But not always, for you can use the same form of writing to accomplish a variety of purposes. You can write a newsletter to describe a new departmental activity or to recommend a new book. You can write a memo to explain a recent administrative decision or to try to persuade someone to do something.

Generally, you write to *describe* something or someone; to *narrate* an order of incidents about an event; to *explain* a situation, a process, or a viewpoint; to *criticize* something or someone; or to *persuade* someone to accept a point of view or a conclusion.

Description

When writing to describe someone or something, concentrate on helping the reader see, hear, smell, taste, and/or feel, depending on what you're trying to describe. Above all, your writing must be clear, concise, and accurate. Expressing detailed, factual information is usually the key to making descriptive writing interesting reading. If you're writing about a person, try to answer such questions as, How does this person sound, walk, dress, smile? What strikes you first about this person? What impresses you about him or her?

If you're describing an inanimate object such as a building, follow a similar line of questioning: What is your first impression of the building? How does it appear up close? from a distance? Is it made of wood or brick or concrete? How many windows does it have? What are their shapes? Does the building have a distinctive color? What feeling does the building give you when you are in it? outside it? How does it relate to other buildings around it? to its natural surroundings?

Specific answers to questions of this sort give life to descriptive writing. Remember, you are trying to evoke several of your reader's senses, not just sight and sound. Make the situation come alive for your reader. One way to check your descriptive writing is to read it aloud. Can you see what you are trying to describe in more than one dimension? Does what you are describing become real?

In writing descriptive material, first decide what kind of impression you want to create. If you work for a small company where you are expected to write a sales brochure about a new product, you need to decide whether to focus on the product's price, beauty, or useful-ness—or on the benefits to the buyer. Once you decide, select examples and details to make your point. Appeal to the reader's senses, as well as intellect, in your descriptive material.

If you operate a nursery and are writing sales literature about a new variety of strawberry plant, you need to decide what appeal to use. If you're writing for the small gardener, what impression do you want to create? Something about the genetic background of this new variety? Probably not. Something about its high yields? its superior taste? its ability to grow in a variety of soils? its brilliant red color? its resistance to disease? Yes, probably all of these, woven into a message that describes the new strawberry variety concisely and draws on a variety of the reader's senses.

Narration

Narrative writing is one of the most common forms of writing. When you fill out an accident report, indicating in detail the direction your car was traveling, the condition of the street, the direction the other car was going, the events leading up to the accident, and the actual account of the accident, you are engaging in narrative writing. Many professionals are required to submit yearly reports of their activities. A police officer reports on the events of a robbery; a social worker writes a case history of a family; an elementary teacher reports the year's progress of his or her class; a sales manager writes about declining sales in a given territory over a three-year period. Each of these persons is engaging in narrative writing.

To do narrative writing, identify what you want to communicate and then arrange the events in the order in which they happened, selecting details that help your reader understand each event. As with descriptive writing, good narration includes many details that help clearly communicate points to the reader. They also help make the writing interesting.

Explanation

You write to explain when you try to help someone understand the background or basic conditions of something—a specific situation, a process, a viewpoint. You write to explain when you try to help someone understand how something works, say a memory typewriter. You write to explain when you try to interpret a law in terms of what it means to your business or department.

Explanatory writing must be as objective as possible and totally accurate. If there are two sides to a question, you must discuss both sides equally.

You can explain something in at least four ways: (1) defining, (2) comparing, (3) contrasting, and (4) analyzing.

Defining

You can explain something by defining it. That seems easy. If you are writing a sociological paper, you define *society.* If you are writing something about computers, you define *computer.* It is not, however, an easy task. Ask any graduate student writing a thesis who must define the terms he or she is using. Some will sweat over the task for hours.

Some writers take the easy way out and use other people's definitions, such as the dictionary's or an expert's. Of course, that is a legitimate approach to defining something. Why spend hours defining something that has already been defined? Writing your own definition may be useful, though, if you want to use a term in a particular way, with a nuance of meaning that the dictionary hasn't included or an expert hasn't considered. Then you're faced with writing your own definition.

One way to write a definition is to write it in the style the dictionary uses—a tightly written, concise statement. A word of caution, though: Never use the word you are defining in its definition. For instance, don't define *belief* as "something that is believed." That tells the reader little.

A second way to define something is to write a concise statement about its various dimensions or components. When I once conducted research about returning students, I defined them as those students twenty-five years or older who had been out of school for three or more years.

Comparing

To help your reader understand something, it often helps to compare it with something already familiar to your reader. For instance, if you're trying to explain the operation of a microcomputer, you can compare its keyboard with a regular typewriter keyboard, showing that in many respects the two are exactly the same.

A close relative of comparison is the analogy. Whereas comparison points out similarities between things in the same class (two keyboards on two different machines, for instance), an analogy points out the similarities between things in different classes. "Influential people in our lives are the sturdy oak trees we rely on" is an analogy.

Contrasting

Another useful way to explain what something is, is to explain what it is *not,* to make a contrast. For instance, when writing about returning students, I contrasted them with the younger, more traditional college-age students. Of course, traditional college-age students and returning students also have much in common. So in writing about the two groups of students, I used both comparison and contrast in the same piece, showing how the groups were similar as well as different.

Comparison and contrast are often used together because both are best used when writing about similar ideas, persons, or situations. For instance, if you were writing an essay about a white oak tree, you would likely want to compare it with other oak trees, pointing out the similarities of all oaks. But to help your reader clearly identify the white oak and understand it as a distinct tree, you would then contrast it with other oaks, pointing out how it was different.

Analyzing

Explaining by analysis is separating a subject into its natural parts and examining each part.

The first step in analysis is to search for the logical components of what you are analyzing and then look carefully at each component. If you were analyzing an electrically powered automobile, you would examine the electric motor, the batteries, the power train, the passenger compartment, and so on. You would examine each component and write an explanation of what you found. Once you completed the analysis of the individual components, you would then write about the entire automobile.

You may be asked to analyze the operations of an office, a set of recommendations, or a report. You may even be asked to analyze the writings of others. The following is a process that is useful for analyzing a book or an article:

1. Read for the overview of the book or the article. Search for the main ideas and the structure of the writing. Chapter titles and subheads are useful clues in determining both the main ideas and the structure. The introductory and summary paragraphs of chapters and major sections of articles often provide strong clues about the main ideas.

2. Determine the overall purpose for the writing and write it down in a sentence or two. List the main ideas and the structure in which they are presented.

3. For each of the main ideas, jot down the questions the author is attempting to answer. What terms does the author use? How are they defined? What answers does the author give to the questions raised?

Criticism

Most of us dislike receiving as well as giving criticism. Both are difficult. Here are some suggestions on how to write two kinds of criticism—criticism of an activity or an event and criticism of a person's performance. These are merely examples of the various kinds of criticism you may be asked to write.

Criticizing an Activity or an Event

Let's say you are writing a criticism of an in-service meeting you attended. You plan to send it to the chairperson of the planning committee. What approach should you use? Your tendency may be to write a blistering letter detailing everything you disliked about the meeting, making certain you select adjectives that will "get the chairperson's attention." You may feel better after you have un-loaded, but what have you accomplished? Criticism should have a positive outcome, or it shouldn't be done. You are writing a criticism because you want to improve future in-service meetings. How can you write a criticism with this purpose in mind?

First, you need to get your emotions under control. Although an emotional outburst may certainly command attention when it is read, it seldom is helpful. Your emotional outburst will often trigger an emotional response from your reader, and little is accomplished that is positive.

Where can you begin in writing this kind of criticism? Begin with an analysis of the meeting. Examine its various components: registra-tion procedures, content, resource people, timing, facilities, and so on. Then make judgments about each component of the meeting. If the resource people, for example, were poorly prepared and couldn't keep the group's attention, say that. Be as specific as you can with evidence to support your judgment. Be firm, be frank, but be fair. It helps little to write, "I've never attended such a poor in-service meet-ing. It was a waste of time." You may indeed feel like writing that, but it will help improve the situation very little. You must separate knowl-edge from opinion in making a judgment.

Write your criticism taking care that you cannot be criticized for the very reasons you are being critical.

Criticizing Performance

For a research project I once conducted, I asked professors at several universities to tell me what they disliked most about university teaching. Every one of them placed evaluating students and giving grades as either the most disliked or the second most disliked thing he or she did.

Giving criticism makes us uncomfortable. Professors fear a criti-cized student will go storming out of their offices, ranting about how unfair the professor has been. Supervisors dislike their employees' telling all their friends what a misguided and uninformed supervisor they have. Yet as Professor James Sparks, a specialist in mental health at the University of Wisconsin–Extension, says, "Criticism is a necessary part of human relationships."[1] Sparks offers these sugges-tions for writing criticism:

1.   Write no criticism that you haven't first discussed with a person face to face or at least over the phone. A written criticism should not come as a surprise. What should be avoided is building up a head of criticism and then unloading it all in one memo. Whatever resentment may have existed between people will only be increased.

2.   Be specific and direct. Don't use a shotgun approach to criticism, blasting vague evaluations at someone.

3.   Assess the quality of the relationship you have with someone before writing the criticism. How you relate to the person you are criticizing will influence how you will write the criticism. If the relationship is positive and trusting, it's often easier to be direct. If the relationship is already strained, your criticism must take this into account.

4.   Strive to make the criticism a problem-solving experience for the person being criticized. Write about the problem, not the person. The criticism should have a positive rather than a negative outcome.

5.   *Report* feelings, don't express them. All criticism includes both factual and feeling components. Expressing feelings when writing criticism means writing such things as, "I am very angry with you." Reporting feelings means saying something like, "I was feeling angry when you did this yesterday."

6.   Consider the timing of the criticism. There are wrong times for criticizing. The middle of a rush job is not the time to hand an employee a memo criticizing him or her for something done poorly last week. Also, criticism shouldn't come so long after something has happened that the person criticized scarcely remembers.

7.   Be sure your intention for giving criticism is clear. The person reading your memo should know immediately that you are unhappy with his term paper or her performance on a particular task and you expect improvement. There should be no doubt about why you are criticizing in the mind of the person receiving the criticism.

Giving and receiving criticism is never easy, for it bruises self-esteem and usually evokes feelings of shock, fear, and anger in the person criticized. Sparks says these are normal feelings and are to be expected. Given all the problems and discomforts, we are nevertheless often faced with the need for criticizing other people. Following some of the principles mentioned above should help, but criticism will never be easy.

Persuasion and Argument

When you try to persuade your readers to accept your point of view or conclusion about something or to do something you suggest, you are writing an argument. The word *argument,* to many people, means a shouting match in which one person tries to overcome another person with a loud voice and ingenious attempts at arousing emotion. Emotion is often part of an argument, but good arguments require that loud voices and emotions be tuned down or turned off.

Basically a good argument comprises the following:

• A brief and concise statement of the problem that needs a solution. The statement should be as objective as possible, avoiding any hint of your position on the problem.

• A brief statement of your solution to the problem. As you shall see below, at times you may choose to save the summary statement for the end of the presentation.

• Recognition of the opponents' position on the question and a carefully written refutation of that position.

• A carefully drawn set of reasons of how you arrived at the answer to the question. Sometimes your argument, your reasons for coming up with your particular point of view, are intermixed with the refutation of the opponents' position.

For most arguments, the answer is not altogether cut and dried. There are usually good and bad points to both your solution and your opponents'. It takes skill to recognize the opposing position without discrediting the position you are trying to develop and argue.

Thomas Berry suggests several procedures for presenting an argument in a logical way, including (1) presenting pertinent evidence, (2) using analogy, (3) using inductive reasoning, and (4) using deductive reasoning.[2]

Pertinent Evidence

You use pertinent evidence when you line up the data that help support the point you're trying to make. For example, a few years ago my family and several neighbors were disturbed about traffic near the neighborhood school. Cars were speeding by in a school zone, and we were concerned a child would be hit. From the traffic department, we were able to obtain traffic counts on the street. From the police department, we got data to show how many people had been stopped for speeding in the school zone. From the crossing guards, we obtained information about the number of near accidents they had observed in the past several months, in which cars had not slowed down for children crossing the street. We presented this information in a written report to the city transportation department as evidence of the need for a traffic light at the intersection. It worked. The traffic light was constructed about six months later.

Analogy

Analogy is seldom used by itself but is incorporated with other techniques. For instance, in the example above, the motorists speeding through the school zone could be compared to race car drivers, the street compared to a race track, and the children to innocent bystanders who must look for a break in the race to scurry across the track.

Analogy can be a very powerful technique, for it helps the reader see what you're saying in different, easily understood terms. It often evokes subtle emotion as well.

Inductive Reasoning

Arguing using inductive reasoning means arguing from the specific to the general. Let's say you're aware that administrative procedures on many college and university campuses confuse students. To argue inductively, you would write about the baffling complexity of the registration procedure for students and about the inadequate methods and services for helping them in the admissions office and the counseling center. You would conclude that the administrative climate could be changed to aid students in registering.

One caution when using the inductive approach: Make certain the evidence you cite represents the situation accurately. If you know of only one or two students who've had difficulty with the registration procedures, you have hardly enough information to generalize about the administrative climate for students on that campus.

Deductive Reasoning

Deductive reasoning starts with the general and moves to the particular. Using the example of students' problems with registration, you would begin a deductive argument by writing, "Colleges and universities should change their registration procedures if they want to help students." Then you would cite your reasons.

The syllogism is the classic way of arguing deductively. It goes like this:

> Major premise: All human beings want freedom.
> Minor premise: I am a human being.
> Conclusion: I want freedom.

EXERCISES

1. Review what you've written the past two weeks. Indicate your purpose for each piece of writing: to describe, narrate, explain, criticize, or persuade. Which type of writing was least difficult for you? Why? Which type was most difficult? Why?
2. Write a letter to a friend or an entry in your Writing Log using at least two of the above purposes in writing. Use facts, details, and evidence in your description, narration, explanation, criticism, or argument.

NOTES

1. James Allen Sparks, "Criticism: Trainer's Disaster or Opportunity," *Training/HRD*, July 1981, p. 74; and James Allen Sparks, *Potshots at the Preacher* (Nashville, Tenn.: Abingdon, 1977).
2. Thomas Elliott Berry, *The Craft of Writing* (New York: McGraw-Hill, 1974), pp. 143–150.

Chapter 7

Making Writing Readable

The *Chronicle of Higher Education* carries a column entitled, "Marginalia," which presents a potpourri of ideas and often highlights mangled communications. For instance, here is part of a memo from a dean.

> There has been some confusion over the new course offering and credit and non-credit equivalents for students in College Skills.
>
> 1. The course description for CS 051 will now become the course description and title for CS 064 (a new number) and CS 064 will be equivalent to four credit hours not six as is the case for CS 051. Please note, this will require all students who have enrolled in CS 051 for the Fall to actually be enrolled in CS 064: we will send a change form through and I trust that the Registrar will be able to make these corrections without the students coming in to do a whole drop/add. We will amend the schedule so that all future students will register for CS 064.
>
> 2. To clarify other areas of confusion, please note:
> CS 041 = 3 credit equivalents
> CS 054 = 4 credit equivalents[1]

We probably all have written memos not too different from this one and then wondered why the message was not understood.

In recent years government, academic, and some business writing has been challenged, scoffed at, and made light of by such notables as William Safire and Edwin Newman. And not without good cause, for much writing in recent years is aptly described as gobbledygook.

Richard Mitchell is particularly concerned about academic writing. As the founder and editor of the *Underground Grammarian,* he constantly pokes at poorly written educational materials. He also blames much of the poor writing of government bureaucrats on their former teachers:

> We imagined at first that the language of ignorance and inanity was the native tongue of bureaucrats and administrators. We were wrong. It took us more than a year, a year spent in scrutinizing vile specimens, to realize that all those silly geese had learned that gabble from the Great Gobblers themselves, those wiggly-wattled, biggety birds, the Teacher-training Turkeys.[2]

What is readable writing? It is writing that is simply written, quickly understood, and interesting to read. Readable writing reflects the concern of the writer for the reader. The writing seeks neither to impress the reader nor to ignore the reader's intelligence.

No magic process exists for making writing readable, though following some guidelines can help. Each piece of writing has its own integrity, its own distinctiveness. As a writer, you must look at each writing project as a one-of-a-kind challenge. If you do, you'll find that the project becomes more interesting for you to write as well as more interesting for others to read.

Why Is Readability a Problem?

The writer's attitude contributes to much of the problem of poor writing. Many writers in academic communities, in business, and in government firmly (and mistakenly) believe that a certain kind of writing is expected of their positions. For example, here is a sentence from a report written by a professor of education who was commenting on an essay.

> Many readers will consider his essay on "The Learning Community" to constitute a classic state of the art piece on thinking about human learning as well as a fully developed prolegomenon to the philosophical foundations of that kind of education which is consonant with the concept of the learning stance.

Your first reaction to that sentence was most likely, "What'd he say?" After reading the sentence two or three times, you probably still don't know what it means. But it surely sounds impressive.

Along with pompous writing, there is also a certain arrogance expressed by many writers. Some writers assume that unless you've had as much training and education as they have, you shouldn't expect to understand their writing. Using jargon is one way to ensure that no one outside your field can understand you. Technical fields have technical terms. Medicine has such terms as *endocrine* and *thrombosis.* Law has *plaintiff* and *tort.* Social science has *random sample* and *survey.*

When you are writing for people who understand these terms, you write in a particular way. But that doesn't mean you cannot write for others as well. It may take a few more examples and explanations, but it is possible to write for a broader audience. And by writing for a broader audience, you communicate more effectively with your peers as well because you are paying more attention to the tenets of good writing.

Carl Sagan recently illustrated how effectively a scientist can communicate to a broader audience. In his best-selling book *Cosmos,* Sagan writes about science and the universe for a wide audience to understand and appreciate. Those scientists who hold an arrogant view criticize such "popularizers" as Sagan for compromising science by making it available to the masses. They believe it is impossible to write for both a trained, scientific audience and the general public.

As noted above, there are times when you will write only for the trained audience. But will the so-called trained audience also read and accept the more popular material? Rudolf Flesch says yes. Flesch asks these questions about simplifying your writing: "What will happen to the readers you had to begin with? Will they resent simplification? Will they feel you are now talking down to them? Will they stop reading you in disgust?

"Not at all. If you don't carry simplification too far into primer style, your old readers will not only stay with you but you'll get more of the same kind; and they'll *read you faster, enjoy it more, understand better,* and *remember longer.*"[3]

Readability Guidelines

1. Write for a specific audience. Think about persons who represent the audience you are writing to, and write to those persons. If you wish to write for a broader audience, focus on persons representing that broader audience. Too often writers have only vague notions about who their readers are. If you are writing a book review for a professional journal in your field, your readers are likely very similar to yourself and your coworkers. Focus on a colleague and imagine you are writing the review for him or her.

Too many writers focus on themselves. They write to impress.

They do this by writing long, involved sentences and using words with several syllables. Unfortunately, they neither impress nor communicate. In the long run, writers who try to follow the guidelines for readable writing *do* impress their readers. Readers want to know what writers have to say, and they want to enjoy finding it out. They do not want to wade through a jungle of tangled sentences and paragraphs, guessing at what is being said.

2.   Use first-degree words. Edward T. Thompson, editor in chief of *Reader's Digest,* says first-degree words are those that immediately bring an image to mind. Second-degree words often have to be translated to first-degree words before they are understood.[4]

First-Degree Terms	Second-Degree Terms
agree, give in	acquiesce
stop, pause	cessation
avoid, go around	circumvent
call off, recall	countermand
send out, distribute	disseminate
talk to	dialogue with
varied, mixed	heterogeneous
house	habitation
start, begin	initiate
smallest, least	minimal
face	countenance
book	volume, tome
prevent, wipe out	obviate
read	peruse
later, afterward	subsequently
clear, certain	unequivocal
waver, be uncertain	vacillate

If you have a choice between a simple, first-degree word and a more complicated word, choose the simpler word. The simpler word is usually more precise as well.

3. Avoid pseudo-technical words and vogue words. One way to spot pseudo-technical words is to look for words that end with the suffixes -al, -ance, -ate, -ion, -ive, and -ize. From a quick reading of some professional educational material, I found behavioral, motivational, instrumental, dialectical, delineation, collaboration, segmentation, randomize, maximize, finalize, and centralize. I'll not trouble you with the translations.

Another whole category of pseudo-technical words comes from changing verbs into nouns. Jefferson Bates calls these smothered verbs.[5] Bates says we smother verbs by adding -ance or -ion. For instance, the verb determine becomes determination; negotiate, negotiation; realize, realization; implement, implementation; and authorize, authorization. When verbs are smothered by turning them into nouns, another verb must be added to the sentence. For instance, we may see the following: "A determination was made by Jones that the stock should be sold." Why not write, "Jones determined that the stock should be sold"?

Why is there such an outpouring of pseudo-technical words in writing today, especially in the social sciences and education? Because the pseudo-technical words come from writers who are concerned that what they have to say isn't all that important, so their language is clothed in confusion.

Vogue words are close relatives of pseudo-technical words. They are the popular words of the day that disappear in a relatively short time but are used, it seems, by everyone during the time they are popular. Some vogue words and phrases used at the time of this writing include bottom line, parameter (meaning "limit"), interface, impact (as a verb), and radical chic.

Vogue words are lazy words. Because everyone uses them, you may believe they communicate well and are easily understood. Not necessarily so. People soon become so tired of vogue words that they become vague words that communicate nothing.

Coined words and phrases can also get in the way of good communication, unless you are an Alvin Toffler. Toffler has invented such terms as future shock, throwaway society, blip culture, and modular man. Future shock has caught on and has become a part of our vocabulary. Toffler's other coined phrases have had less acceptance. For most writers, though, it is good advice to steer clear of coined words. Readers react to coined words in a variety of ways, from viewing them as cute to believing the writer is trying to be pretentious. Both may be correct.

Jargon and technical words are a part of every profession and field. It's easy to become complacent and toss them around as if everyone should understand them or be impressed with what you know. Be careful of words that relate specifically to a given profession or field. If you are writing to an audience broader than that field, either avoid using jargon or make sure such words are translated.

4. Emphasize the active voice. Which of the following sentences is more interesting and easier to read: "The ball was caught by the outfielder" or "The outfielder caught the ball"? The first sentence illustrates the passive voice, the second the active. Most people find the active voice more interesting and easier to read. The active voice follows the subject-verb-object pattern. First the actor, then the action, and then what is acted upon.

Unfortunately, much academic and formal writing puts too much emphasis on the passive voice. We often read sentences like this: "Extensive educational possibilities in both rural and urban community development efforts were described by Biddle and Biddle." Or "Longitudinal efforts to study change through education were documented by Franklin." Why not write, "Biddle and Biddle described extensive educational possibilities in both rural and urban community development efforts," or "Franklin documented longitudinal efforts to study change through education"? The sentences are not only easier to read, but they also require fewer words.

The only time it makes sense to use the passive voice is when the person or thing doing the acting is unknown, when the person or thing being acted upon is more important than the actor, or when you want to vary your sentence structure in a paragraph. For instance, the actor is not stated in the following sentence: "Fifteen years ago the goals of Indian agriculture were clearly set out." For purposes of the report, it wasn't important for the reader to know the author of Indian agricultural goals. It is also appropriate to write, "The chairperson of the board was struck by a bicycle," rather than "A bicycle struck the chairperson of the board" (assuming, of course, that the chairperson of the board is more important than the bicycle).

EXERCISE

Rewrite the following sentences using the active voice.

1. More attention to the linking of adult education with adult development is given by adult educators.
2. The report was written by the supervisor.
3. The position paper was prepared by the special committee.
4. The supply cabinet has been left unlocked by someone.
5. Universities are looked to by society to provide leadership.

POSSIBLE ANSWERS

1. Adult educators give more attention to the linking of adult education with adult development.
2. The supervisor wrote the report.
3. The special committee prepared the position paper.
4. Someone left the supply cabinet unlocked.
5. Society looks to universities to provide leadership.

5.   Be precise. It may take a little more time to find exactly the right word, but almost right is not good enough when you're trying to communicate effectively. Of course, to write with precision, you must know exactly what you want to say. If you know exactly what you want to say and find the proper word or combination of words, the chances of your reader's understanding you increase greatly.

For instance, if you write, "John went to Chicago," you are less than precise. Did he drive, walk, hitchhike, fly, or what? Not only does using the precise word make for more precise writing, but it also makes for more interesting writing. The verb *went* is a weak verb showing little action.

For precise writing, you must also be aware of the order of words. Keep related elements of a sentence together and place modifiers as close as possible to the words they are intended to modify. Words like *only* must be watched very carefully. Notice the different meanings of these three sentences because *only* is in different positions: "Only John and Mary received Bs in chemistry" (John and Mary were the only ones in their class to receive Bs); "John and Mary received only Bs in chemistry" (apparently they were expecting a higher grade); "John and Mary received Bs only in chemistry" (they received different grades in their other courses).

To be precise, avoid generalizations. For instance, don't write, "She was unhappy with conditions in the office," when the truth of the matter was she was unhappy with how her supervisor divided the work load. Don't write, "He came late to work." Write, "He came to work half an hour late."

EXERCISE

Rewrite the following sentences to rid them of misplaced modifiers.

1. While climbing the stairs, a new idea popped into John's head.
2. Flying at half-mast, my heart grew sad when I saw the flag.
3. The job was selling boxes of candy to children with prizes in them.
4. The police officer told the frightened couple what they were doing wrong with a smile.
5. There was a rosebush behind the pile of trash that was very beautiful.
6. There should be a letter written by the boss in your mailbox.

POSSIBLE ANSWERS

1. A new idea popped into John's head while he was climbing the stairs. Or, While John was climbing the stairs, a new idea popped into his head.
2. My heart grew sad when I saw the flag flying at half-mast.
3. The job was selling boxes of candy with prizes in them to children.
4. With a smile, the police officer told the frightened couple what they were doing wrong.
5. There was a beautiful rosebush behind the pile of trash.
6. There should be a letter in your mailbox written by the boss. Or, In your mailbox should be a letter written by the boss.

6. Eliminate extra words. Often writers use more words than are needed or one long sentence instead of two shorter ones. For instance, this thirty-word sentence is from a research report:

> The purpose of this study was to examine the extent of the relationship between participation in a program of continuing nursing education and change in professional practice by nurse participants.

A rewrite could be: "Does nursing practice change when a nurse enrolls in a continuing education course? Here is what one study revealed" (nineteen words—both sentences).

Wordiness also results from using roundabout phrases. Many times a roundabout phrase can be translated into one or two words.

Roundabout Phrase	Direct
along the lines of	like
as a result of	because
as of this date	today
call your attention to the fact that	remind you
did not remember	forgot
meets with our approval	we approve
at the present time	now
in order to	to
in the event of	if
in view of the fact that	since
on the subject of	about
from the point of view of	for
in a position to	can, may
for the reason that	because
in advance of, prior to	before
we are writing to ask that you send	please send
for the purpose of	for
on a few occasions	occasionally
on the basis of	by
in the amount of	for
in relation to	about
in a number of cases	some
on behalf	for

Another kind of wordiness is redundancy—writing two words that mean the same thing, usually in the hope that the message will have more impact. Unfortunately, redundancy usually results in fogging the mind and slowing down the reader, who must wade through unnecessary words to find out what is meant.

The following are examples. The words in parentheses can be eliminated without changing the meaning.

(actual) truth	fall (down)
(honest) truth	start (up)
(absolutely) completely	(necessary) requirement
(active) consideration	assemble (together)
big (in size)	scrutinize (carefully)
refer (back)	(two equal) halves
gather (together)	(completely) filled
(first) began	(repeat) again

Other words that can often be eliminated include *of, one, whole, own,* and *very.* For instance, the italicized word(s) in each of the following sentences can be dropped without changing the meaning: "All *of* the graduates found jobs." "This book is *an* interesting *one.*" "She spent the *whole* summer in Europe." "He described his *own* house." "The skyscraper was *very* tall." "He read the manuscript *very* carefully."

It's possible to be too concise with your writing. You must always ask, Does what I have written say what I want it to say? A good check is to ask the questions a journalist asks: Does my writing say who or what is involved? Does it say where? Does it say when? Does it say why? Does it say how?

EXERCISE

Rewrite the following sentences to eliminate wordiness.

1. As a result of your request, we are giving active consideration to your plan. (14 words)

2. In view of the fact that Aristotle isn't alive today, I am not in a position to say much about how he would view our society. (26 words)
3. I'd like to call your attention to the fact that our orders have decreased by 10 percent during the past year. (21 words)
4. In the event that students complete the necessary requirements for graduation in advance of the normal time, they may graduate early. (21 words)

POSSIBLE ANSWERS

1. At your request we are considering your plan. (8 words)
2. Since Aristotle isn't alive today, I cannot say how he would view our society. (14 words)
3. I remind you that our orders have decreased by 10 percent the past year. (14 words)
4. If students complete requirements before the normal time, they may graduate early. (12 words)

7. Link paragraphs with transitions. Paragraphs are often referred to as the building blocks of writing. Transitions are the mortar that holds the building blocks together. Transitions help your readers move from idea to idea without becoming lost; they help prepare your reader for what's coming. Following are transitions for particular situations:

When offering a reason: *because, therefore*
When offering additional reasons: *in addition, also, moreover*
When introducing an example: *for instance, for example*
When introducing a contrast: *in contrast, however, unlike*
When introducing a sequence: *first, second, next*
When making a time shift: *before, then, afterward*
When making an idea shift: *however, but, or, nevertheless*
When introducing a conclusion: *to sum up, therefore, thus*

8. Keep the average length of sentences short. Shorter sentences are much easier to read. How short should sentences be? For general reading, an average of eighteen to twenty words per sentence is a good goal to shoot for. Some sentences will be shorter, some longer. When your writing begins to average thirty words per sentence or more, it becomes increasingly difficult to read and understand.

For example, this sentence was found in a philosophy book:

> To be sure, unlike over-specialization, the constriction of awareness produced by training is something aimed at deliberately by those who engage in the training; moreover, while it may be undertaken for good or bad purposes, and be well or ill done, the notion of "training," unlike that of "over-specialization," is not the notion of something per se undesirable, perhaps because training, unlike over-specialization, does not necessarily deter the learner from subsequently exploring and responding to those dimensions of knowledge and experience which the process of training nevertheless itself by definition neglects (for example, the wider scientific and social aspects of telecommunications which are by definition excluded from anything we should call the mere "training" of a telephonist, but which a telephonist is unlikely to be positively *deterred* by his training from appreciating if he should ever be subsequently led to consider them); and so, although clearly processes of "training" have to be sharply distinguished from processes of "education," unlike "over-specialization" the notion of "training" is not the notion of something which is positively *incompatible* with a man's pursuit of education in the full meaning of the term.[6]

That one sentence uses 187 words. It flies right off the scales in terms of readability. And it isn't just the length that makes the sentence difficult to read, but also the number of modifiers and clauses introduced. Such long sentences are also extremely complex sentences. Long sentences are difficult to write without tangling ideas with each other, misplacing modifiers, and generally confusing the reader (if not the writer).

9. Concentrate on tone and rhythm. You can follow all the guidelines discussed in this chapter and still lose your readers if you have not considered the tone and rhythm of your writing.

Tone is the kind of feeling that writing evokes in readers. How you use words, write sentences, and organize paragraphs creates a tone, or feeling. And how your readers feel about your writing often makes the difference in whether they continue reading.

Unfortunately, much writing these days often creates a tone of aloofness and arrogance. For instance, here is a statement from a summary of completed research projects:

> This information provides for a comparative analysis of discrepancies in expectations within and among groups central to the program, and

discrepancies between current practice and various perspectives of those most directly involved in policy formation and program administration.

The tone is pompous and arrogant, and besides, the sentence makes little sense. A plain tone, unadorned with contrived pseudo-technical terms, not only creates a positive feeling in the reader, but it is also much more easily understood.

Creating a rhythm in your writing also helps keep the reader reading. Rhythm helps make writing interesting, which is one of the requisites for making writing readable.

One way to create rhythm is to vary the length of sentences and paragraphs. Mix short ones with long ones. And vary the construction of sentences. Start them in different ways. For instance, you could write either, "Many people enjoy discussing politics," or "Discussing politics is something many people enjoy." The passive voice can be used to break the monotony of similar sentence construction, but if used too often, it interferes with readability.

Parallelism is another technique for adding rhythm to your writing. Parallelism means putting words, phrases, clauses, and sentences into a *balanced grammatical structure.* Words are balanced with words, phrases with phrases, and so on. For example, "On my farm I grow wheat, corn, and sometimes I grow soybeans" sounds awkward. But "On my farm I grow wheat, corn, and sometimes soybeans" is parallel and rhythmic.

One way to check the tone and rhythm of your writing is to read it aloud. Which words or phrases nag at you and slow down your reading? Which words or phrases don't sound right to your ear? Those are likely the rough spots you need to work on.

If you have trouble "hearing" your writing while you are reading it, read it into a tape recorder and then play it back and listen. The rough spots, the places where the tone and rhythm are wrong, will jump out at you.

   10. Use dialogue. Fiction writers use dialogue extensively. Dialogue can also be a useful tool for making nonfiction writing more readable.

For example, here is how John McPhee used dialogue when he reported on Theodore Taylor, a nuclear physicist and atomic-bomb designer:

Driving around Los Alamos with him once, when I went along on a visit he made there in 1972, I asked him what he had done to occupy himself during the flat periods between projects, the lulls that would come in any pattern of conceptual work. He said, "Between bombs, we messed around, in one way or another. We bowled snowballs the size of volleyballs down the E Building corridor to see what would happen. We played shuffleboard with icicles." He supposed it helped relieve the tension, of which there was a fair amount from time to time.[7]

Quoting people breaks up writing and makes it easier to read. Dialogue also makes writing more interesting because real people have said the words.

Dialogue may present some problems for the writer, though, particularly if people are quoted directly from interviews. When people talk, they are wordy. They repeat themselves, change ideas in mid-sentence, and add little extras that make no sense when transcribed. So when you use dialogue from interviews, condense the spoken words to fit your requirements.

Readability Scales

A technical approach to determine readability uses one of several systems for analyzing writing and computing a readability score.

For instance, Robert Gunning has developed a "fog index."[8] It works this way:

Select a medium-length paragraph from your writing (about 150 words long, counting numbers and dates as single words). Count both the number of words and the number of sentences. Divide the number of words by the number of sentences to obtain the average number of words per sentence.

Next, look at your sample paragraph and note all the words with three or more syllables. Don't count compound words, such as *buttonhole,* or words that begin with capital letters, such as names of people and places. Also exclude the first word of each sentence.

When you have counted all words with three or more syllables, add that number to the average number of words per sentence and multiply the total by 0.4. The resulting number will correspond to the reading comprehension grade level. For example, if you come up with an eight, it means that someone with an eighth-grade education can understand your writing.

To find out if your writing is interesting to read, apply the Flesch "Human Interest Formula":[9]

Select a sample of 100 words. Count the personal words, or pronouns such as *she, he, them, you* (but not *it* or a plural pronoun referring to things).

Count all the words that imply gender, such as *mother, brother, father, businessman,* and all proper names.

Count collective nouns such as *family* and *group.*

Count the personal sentences: those containing dialogue set off with quotation marks, references beginning with "he said" or "she said," sentences that directly question or command the reader to do something, or sentences that are exclamations.

Once you've counted the personal words and the personal sentences, multiply the personal words in the 100-word sample by 3.635. Multiply the personal sentences by .314. Add the products, and you have your human interest score. The lower the number, the more dull and uninteresting your writing. "Interesting" begins around 25 or 30; "highly interesting" is over 50. A score lower than 10 means "deadly dull."

EXERCISES

1. Review the early entries you made in your Writing Log and apply the ten principles for making writing readable. In which areas did you have problems? Do the same thing with recent entries. Have you improved?
2. Select any required writing you've done recently. Apply the Gunning and the Flesch formulas. What are your reactions to your scores?
3. After completing exercises 1 and 2, determine in which areas you need further work to improve the readability of your writing. Jot them down in your Writing Log, and refer to them from time to time.

NOTES

1. "Marginalia," *Chronicle of Higher Education,* vol. 22, no. 10, April 27, 1981.
2. From the December 1979 issue of the *Underground Grammarian,* quoted in the *Chronicle of Higher Education,* vol. 22, no. 10, April 27, 1981, p. 16.
3. Rudolf Flesch, *The Art of Readable Writing* (New York: Harper & Row, 1974), p. 175.
4. Edward T. Thompson, "How to Write Clearly," *Power of the Printed Word* (Elmsford, N.Y.: International Paper Company, 1979).

5. Jefferson Bates, *Writing with Precision* (Washington, D.C.: Acropolis Books, 1978), p. 22.
6. R. W. K. Paterson, *Values, Education, and the Adult* (Boston: Routledge & Kegan Paul, 1979), p. 182.
7. John McPhee, *The Curve of Binding Energy* (New York: Farrar, Straus and Giroux, 1973, 1974), p. 114.
8. Robert Gunning, *The Techniques of Clear Writing* (New York: McGraw-Hill, 1952).
9. Rudolf F. Flesch, "A New Readability Yardstick," *Journal of Applied Psychology* 32 (June 1948): 221–233.

Chapter 8

Knowing the Mechanics of English

Building contractors can choose from a wide variety of building materials—brick or stone, concrete or wood, steel or plastic. How well a building looks and is constructed depends on how skillfully the materials are chosen and assembled. Some materials go well together. They support the building and at the same time are aesthetically pleasing. Other materials may support the building but don't look quite right when put together. And still others may look good but result in construction that collapses under its own weight.

So it is with writers and writing. Writers have access to the building materials of language—words, sentences, and paragraphs. Choosing these materials carefully and putting them together with skill make the difference among poor, average, and truly outstanding writing.

One chapter is not enough to cover the basics of word usage, spelling, grammar, and punctuation (refer to chapter 14 for a list of references that cover these topics in greater depth). What it can do, though, is focus on common problems many writers face.

Writing is made up of words—short words and long words, common words and technical words. To write well, you must become a master of words. You must know exactly the right word to use. You must know how each word contributes to what you are trying to say.

101

Parts of Speech

Before examining a few of the problems writers face, let's review the eight parts of speech. They are nouns, verbs, adjectives, adverbs, conjunctions, prepositions, pronouns, and interjections.

The same word may occasionally be used as different parts of speech at different times. In one sentence, a word might be used as a noun; in another, as a verb. One key to understanding word use is to answer the question, What is this word's function in this particular sentence?

Nouns

Nouns name persons, places, objects, ideas, qualities, and actions. **Common** nouns name classes of persons or things: *man, building.* **Proper** nouns name particular persons, places, or things: *Thomas Jefferson, Milwaukee, Empire State Building.* They begin with capital letters. **Abstract** nouns name qualities or general ideas: *enthusiasm, spirit.* **Collective** nouns name groups considered as units: *flock, audience, industry.* In addition, nouns have number; that is, they are singular or plural.

Verbs

Verbs express action ("John *jogged* to school") or a state of being ("Mary's job *is* boring"). Some verbs are auxiliary, or helping, verbs; they are used to help form other verbs. Helping verbs include *be, can, could, do, have, may, might, must, should, will* (for example, *can* drive, *could* run, *must* sleep, *will* expire). Other verbs are linking verbs; they connect parts of a sentence (for example, "John *appeared* tired," "The professor *seems* young"). Some common linking verbs are *appear, look, seem, become, feel, taste.*

Adjectives

Adjectives describe, limit, or in some way make the meaning of nouns and pronouns more exact. Adjectives may be descriptive (a *tall* tree, a *yellow* house), limiting (*five* concerts, a *former* job), or proper (*Wisconsin* cheese, *American* slang). Adjectives can answer the question of what kind (an *excellent* proposal) or how many (*twenty-four* books).

Adverbs

Adverbs modify verbs, adjectives, or other adverbs. Adverbs answer the questions of why, where, when, how, and to what extent: "She *rarely* called" (*rarely* modifies the verb *called* and answers the question of when); "His report was *too* short" (*too* modifies the adjective *short* and answers the question of to what extent); "He *practically* never wins" (*practically* modifies the adverb *never* and helps answer the question of when).

Conjunctions

Conjunctions connect words, phrases, or clauses. **Coordinating** conjunctions connect words, phrases, or clauses of equal rank. Coordinating conjunctions include *and, but, or,* and *nor* (beans *and* corn, tall *but* thin, sweet *or* sour). **Subordinating** conjunctions connect dependent clauses with main clauses. Subordinating conjunctions include *when, since, because, where, after, before, if, though,* and *while* ("According to the latest report, the price of sugar rose *when* frost hit Louisiana," "*Since* he sprained his ankle, John no longer jogs to work"). **Correlative** conjunctions are used in pairs: *both . . . and, whether . . . or (not), either . . . or, neither . . . nor, not only . . . but also, so . . . as.*

Prepositions

Prepositions show the relationship between certain words in a sentence. The word *preposition* comes from the Latin for "a placing before," which means a preposition is placed before a noun or a pronoun. Prepositions always have an object. For example, in the sentence "This computer is for word processing," *for* is the preposition and *word processing* the object of the preposition. *For word processing* is called a prepositional phrase. The preposition *for* shows the relationship between *computer* and *word processing*.

Some common words used as prepositions include *at, from, in, of, to,* and *on.*

Pronouns

Pronouns substitute for nouns. The word *pronoun* means "for a noun"; thus, every pronoun used in a sentence must refer directly to a noun (the antecedent of the pronoun). In the sentence "Jane drove her car to work," *her* is the pronoun and *Jane* the antecedent. Common pronouns include *I, me, he, us,* and *you.*

Interjections

Interjections are exclamatory words used to express strong feelings. They have no direct grammatical relation to other words in a sentence. Interjections include words used only as interjections, such as *oh, ouch,* and *whew,* as well as words that may also be used as other parts of speech, such as *goodness, well,* and *my.* Interjections are often followed by an exclamation point (*"Well!* I see you're flunking again," *"Oh!* I didn't know you were standing behind me").

Common Problems

I make no attempt to include all the many grammatical problems writers face, but some of the more common ones follow.

Forming Plurals

How many times have you seen, "TV is a media that we simply can't trust anymore," or "This data shows that . . ."? *Media* is the plural form of *medium,* and *data* of *datum.* Thus, to be correct, you should say, "TV is a medium that we . . ." and "These data show that . . ." (or "This datum shows that" if referring to only one number). Other plural forms that often give writers problems follow.

Singular	Plural
addendum	addenda
alumnus	alumni
analysis	analyses
axis	axes
bacterium	bacteria
basis	bases
crisis	crises
criterion	criteria
hypothesis	hypotheses
memorandum	memoranda
parenthesis	parentheses

synopsis	synopses
synthesis	syntheses
thesis	theses

The plural forms of proper names give some writers problems. For most names, add an *s* to make the name plural (*Smith, Smiths; Corrigan, Corrigans*). When the name ends in *s, x, ch, sh,* or *z,* add *es* to form the plural:

Singular	Plural
Mr. and Mrs. Jones	the Joneses
Mr. and Mrs. Maddox	the Maddoxes
Mr. and Mrs. Karch	the Karches
Mr. and Mrs. Walsh	the Walshes
Mr. and Mrs. Patz	the Patzes

Do *not* use an apostrophe to indicate the plural of a name (*the Jones'* or *the Higgens'*).

Use an apostrophe to form the plurals of abbreviations with periods ("No C.O.D.'s"), lowercase letters used as nouns ("Mind your p's and q's"), and capital letters that would be confusing if *s* alone were added ("She received all A's last term").

EXERCISE

For each of the following sentences, determine whether the correct form (singular or plural) of the italicized word is used. If it is correct, write *correct.* If incorrect, write the correct form.

1. He met with the *Joneses* last evening.
2. A meeting of the college *alumnus* was scheduled for Saturday.
3. The correct *criteria* for this decision was number one.
4. *Smiths* are found everywhere in the United States.
5. Professor Anderson conducted twelve *analysis* of the problem.
6. The *synopses* of the book was well written.
7. The *Lenox'* are a most interesting couple.
8. Graduate students in English completed ten *thesis* last year.

9. Six *M.S.'s* and three *Ph.D.'s* were awarded.
10. Many schools are returning to the three *R's*.

ANSWERS

---

1. correct   2. alumni   3. criterion   4. correct   5. analyses
6. synopsis   7. Lenoxes   8. theses   9. correct   10. Rs

First Person, Second Person, Third Person

Person refers to the perspective from which you are writing. First-person writing is from the perspective of the writer ("I want to say this," "My position is . . ." "We see things this way"). Second-person writing is used when addressing someone directly ("You should do this," "You're the one who counts"). Third-person writing is used when writing about someone or something ("He thinks differently today," "They often do those things," "It's a new world").

A common error for many writers is mixing several different perspectives within the same paragraph, sometimes even within the same sentence. This leads to disjointed, confusing writing. For example, consider the following short paragraph:

"I want to describe how to play baseball. You first hit the ball. Then the batter runs as fast as possible to first base."

The first sentence is written in first person, the second in second person, and the third in third person.

EXERCISE

Rewrite the entire paragraph about baseball in (1) first person, (2) second person, and (3) third person.

POSSIBLE ANSWERS

---

1. I want to describe how to play baseball. First I hit the ball. Then I run as fast as I can to first base.
2. Here's how you play baseball. First you hit the ball. Then you run as fast as you can to first base.

3. Baseball is played this way. The batter first hits the ball. Then he or she runs as fast as possible to first base.

Problems with Adjectives and Adverbs

Comparisons

For most adjectives and adverbs of one syllable, form the comparative by adding *er* ("Of the two buildings on the block, the insurance building is the *taller*") and the superlative by adding *est* ("Of the three buildings on the block, the insurance building is the *tallest*").

Generally, for adjectives and adverbs of more than one syllable, form the comparative by adding the word *more* or *less* to the adjective or adverb: "Jim is *more* competent than Bill." Form the superlative by adding the word *most* or *least*: "Of the three of them, Bill is the *most* competent."

Adverbs with Two Forms

Many of the most commonly used adverbs have two forms (*fair, fairly; short, shortly; quick, quickly; slow, slowly; direct, directly*). For instance: "She doesn't play *fair*." "He will be home *fairly* soon." In the first example, *fair* describes how the person plays; in the second example, *fairly* helps answer the question of when.

Confusing the Adjective with the Adverb

Use an adverb when the word following a verb refers to the action of the verb: "He walked *slowly*" (not *slow*). But use an adjective when the word following a verb refers to the subject of the sentence: "The manager got *lucky*" (*lucky* describes the manager).

Some writers tangle adjectives and adverbs when writing about looking, feeling, tasting, smelling, and hearing. For example, which of the following is correct: "The perfume smells sweet" or "The perfume smells sweetly"? From a quick reading, many would say both sentences are correct. But look more carefully. In the first sentence, *sweet* is an adjective that modifies the noun *perfume*. In the second sentence, *sweetly* is an adverb and thus must modify the verb *smells*. But perfume can't smell anything. Thus, the second sentence is incorrect.

The rule to follow: When the word modifies a noun, use the adjective; when the word modifies an action being performed, use the adverb.

EXERCISE

If the italicized word or words in each sentence are correct, write *correct.* If incorrect, write the correct form.

1. Of the two men, John was the *tallest.*
2. Jane was *more thin* than Earl.
3. Temperatures are *more warmer* in Florida than in Wisconsin.
4. The car felt *warmly.*
5. The bus stopped *short.*
6. I will be along *shortly.*
7. Of the three flavors, I like vanilla *best.*
8. Pauline is *more beautiful* than Susan.
9. Mary's perfume smelled *sensuously.*
10. The professor walks *slow.*

ANSWERS

1. taller   2. thinner   3. drop *more*   4. warm   5. correct
6. correct   7. correct   8. correct   9. sensuous   10. slowly

Problems with Verbs

Because verbs correctly chosen can show action and movement, they help make writing understandable and certainly more interesting to read.

Agreement

Basically, verbs and subjects should agree in person and number. A mistake in agreement often stems from not knowing what the subject of the sentence is because a word, a phrase, or even a clause is placed between the subject and the verb. You must determine what the subject is and make the verb agree: "The *condition* of these twelve people *is* complicated." "The *box* of books that you ordered *was* delivered today."

Compound subjects require the plural form of the verb: "Mary and Jane *sing* in the choir." "The director and the assistant director *run* the show." The only exception to this rule is when two subjects connected by *and* are commonly seen as a unit. When this occurs, use the singular verb: "Bacon and eggs *is* his favorite breakfast."

When two subjects are connected by *and* but are the same individual, the singular form of the verb should be used. The form of the verb lets the reader know whether one or two people are involved: "The president and chairperson of the board *is* coming to the banquet" (the president is also chairperson of the board).

When singular subjects are connected by *or* or *nor,* the subject is considered singular and takes a singular verb: "Neither Pete nor Tom *is* responsible." In such uses, the singular "one" is understood.

When two subjects are connected by *or* or *nor* and one of them is plural, the one closest to the verb dictates whether the verb is singular or plural: "Either the horse or the cows *go.*" "Either the cows or the horse *goes.*"

Indefinite pronouns such as *another, one, neither, anyone, each,* and *either* always take singular verbs: "Neither of the two *is* any good." "Each of the members of Congress *votes* often."

When phrases begin with *one of,* use a singular verb: "One of us *has* to win this game." "One of the people involved *is* missing."

Splitting Infinitives

To split or not to split, that is the question. For years it was a mortal sin for any writer to split an infinitive, yet there are times when a split helps improve communication.

An infinitive is a verb form preceded by the word *to,* such as *to run, to see, to climb.* You split the infinitive when you write *to quickly run, to clearly see, to briskly climb.* You avoid splitting the infinitive when you write *to run quickly, to see clearly, to climb briskly.*

In most cases, it is best to avoid splitting an infinitive. But a grammatical rule borrowed from Latin may sometimes be broken to make an English sentence clearer. Split an infinitive only when you want to avoid an awkward, unnatural construction. Consider the following: "To better introduce myself to the situation . . ." versus "To introduce better myself . . ." The second, "correct" form is clumsy and confusing.

EXERCISE

If the italicized word or words in each sentence are correct, write *correct.* If incorrect, write the correct form.

1. The problem for many students *are* grades.
2. Tom *don't* study nearly enough.

3. Pete, Tom, and everyone in purchasing *was* fired today.
4. He tried *to gracefully apologize.*
5. Either the state university or the community colleges *are* considered for closing.
6. Either the community colleges or the state university *are* considered for closing.
7. The leader and president of this group *are* representing us in Milwaukee. (One person is both leader and president.)
8. Neither Joe nor Ruth *are* responsible for the overdraft.
9. One of the best ways to win approval *is* to work hard.
10. Each of forty samples *were* contaminated.

ANSWERS

1. is 2. doesn't 3. were 4. to apologize gracefully 5. correct
6. is 7. is 8. is 9. correct 10. was

Problems with Possessives

Use an apostrophe and an *s* to show the possessives of most nouns: *Sue's violin, today's interest rate, a master's degree.* To show the possessive of a singular noun ending with an *s*, you may choose between optional styles. Many writers use an apostrophe and *s* only when the pronunciation of the second *s* sound is expected: *the boss's chair, Gus's sister, Dickens' story.* Others use an apostrophe and *s* for all singular nouns except *Jesus, Moses,* and Greek names ending with *es*: *Dickens's story, Jesus' example, Socrates' death.* Whichever style you choose, use it consistently.

For a plural noun that does not end with an *s*, simply add the apostrophe and *s*: *men's shirts, children's toys.* For a plural noun that ends with an *s*, add only the apostrophe: *boys' games, students' records.* The words *his, hers, its, ours, yours, theirs,* and *whose* are already possessive and thus do not require an apostrophe: "Each item is mailed in *its* own carton" (*it's* is the contraction for *it is*). "*Whose* book is it?" (*who's* is the contraction for *who is*).

Don't confuse the plural form with the possessive form: *Ms. Jones's car* (possessive), *the Joneses* (plural), *the Joneses' car* (plural possessive).

EXERCISE

If the italicized word in each sentence is correct, write *correct*. If incorrect, write the correct form.

1. *Mabels'* car needs tuning.
2. The *alumni's* records were mailed.
3. *It's* record is not clear.
4. *Moses'* teachings influenced many.
5. The *witness'* bills were excessive.

ANSWERS

1. Mabel's   2. correct   3. Its   4. correct   5. witness's

Agreement Between Pronouns and Nouns

A pronoun refers directly to a noun and must be in agreement with the noun (its antecedent) in number: "All of the *workers* were waiting for *their* checks" (the antecedent *workers* is plural). "A *student* has all the time *he or she* wants" (the antecedent *student* is singular).

Two or more antecedents joined by *and* require a plural pronoun: "Tom and Jenny have completed *their* graduate degrees." Two or more singular antecedents joined by *or* or *nor* require a singular pronoun: "Neither machine A nor machine B has completed *its* work."

Problems with Word Usage

Below are examples of word groups that often give writers problems. When you discover a word that is a problem for you, look it up in a dictionary and write its definition on a card. The only way to avoid errors with problem words is to learn their correct use.

Affect-effect. Affect is usually a verb meaning "to influence; to impress": "Heinrich's writing *affects* me greatly." *Effect* can be a verb or a noun. As a verb, it means "to bring about; to execute": "The professor *effected* the college's decision." As a noun, it means "impression, result, fulfillment, or accomplishment": "You will long remember the *effects* of your schooling."

Amount-number. Amount refers to things in bulk: "There is a large *amount* of wheat." *Number* refers to individual items: "There is a large *number* of students."

Between-among. In most instances, use *between* when referring to two persons or things ("Few differences exist *between* A and B") and *among* when referring to more than two persons or things ("Few disagreements exist *among* the three of them").

Bring-take. Bring means "to carry or to come with something toward" the speaker: "*Bring* me the report." *Take* is the opposite. It means "to move something away from" the speaker: "*Take* this to Sam's office."

Compare-contrast. Compare to refers to pointing out likenesses between objects in different classes: "*Compare* oaks *to* skyscrapers." *Compare with* refers to pointing out likenesses or differences between objects in the same class: "*Compare* oaks *with* willows." *Contrast* refers to pointing out differences: "*Contrast* oaks with willows."

Complement-compliment. Complement means that something belongs with or goes well with something else: "His necktie *complements* his suit well." *Compliment* means "to praise or flatter": "She *complimented* him on a job well done."

Consul-council-counsel. A consul is an official who represents his or her country in a foreign country. A council is an assembly of people. *Counsel* can mean "advice" ("He gave thoughtful *counsel* to everyone"), "an adviser" ("She was the *counsel* of many"), or "to give advice" ("He *counseled* her on many matters").

Discover-invent. Discover means "to find something that was there before one came": "Pete *discovered* an arrowhead in his backyard." *Invent* means "to create something new": "Nancy *invented* a way to study more efficiently."

Farther-further. Farther refers to an actual distance: "The two cities were *farther* apart than I thought." *Further* refers to a figurative distance, a greater degree or a greater extent: "The two men were *further* apart in their ideas than many imagined."

Fewer-less. Fewer applies to a number: "We have *fewer* dollars than we had last year." *Less* applies to a degree or an amount: "We have *less* money than we had last year."

Formally-formerly. Formally means "in accordance with established rules or customs": "She dressed *formally* for the dance." *Formerly* means "at an earlier time": "He *formerly* served as secretary."

Good-well. Good is an adjective: "His writing is *good.*" *Well* is an adverb or, when referring to health, an adjective: "She works as *well* as she is able." "John feels *well* again."

Last-latest. Last means "final": "Everyone listened to his *last* words." *Latest* means "most recent": "Her *latest* book is a best-seller."

Latter-last. Latter refers to the second of two items mentioned: "Considering books one and two, the *latter* is more interesting." *Last* refers to the final item when more than two are mentioned: "Of fall, winter, and spring, I prefer the *last.*"

Principal-principle. Principal as a noun can mean "the chief person": "He was the *principal* in the case." *Principle* is always a noun. It means "a rule, a belief, a truth, or a policy": "She would never compromise her *principles.*"

Precede-proceed. Precede means "to go before": "He *preceded* me in this office." *Proceed* means "to go forward": "Let's *proceed* with the plan."

Raise-raze-rise. Raise means "to lift; to elevate": "Mary *raised* her hand." *Raze* means "to tear down": "The Smiths *razed* their store building." *Rise* means "to get oneself up or move oneself up": "*Rise* up and greet the new day."

Respectfully-respectively. Respectfully means "in a way showing honor or respect": "The minutes are *respectfully* submitted." *Respectively* means "in the previously specified order": "Claude, Mae, and Pete received an A, a B, and a C on the test *respectively.*"

Stationary-stationery. Stationary means "remaining in one place": "He stood *stationary* for twenty minutes." *Stationery* refers to paper for writing: "Some writers prefer colored *stationery.*"

To-too. To is a preposition: "José goes *to* work." *Too* means "also": "Mary goes to work *too.*"

Unabridged-abridged. Unabridged means "of full length; not cut." *Abridged* means "reduced or cut." An unabridged dictionary is complete. An abridged dictionary is one that has been shortened but contains essential information.

Uninterested-disinterested. Uninterested means "not interested": "Many observers were *uninterested* in the game." *Disinterested* means "impartial": "The umpire was a *disinterested* party in the game."

EXERCISE

If the italicized word in each sentence is correct, write *correct.* If incorrect, write the correct word.

1. The *affects* of the drug wore off slowly.
2. The *number* of doctors increased each year.
3. Mary, *bring* this camera with you when you go to Europe.
4. The *principle's* car had a flat tire.
5. She was *formally* a clerk.
6. *Fewer* people have applied this year.
7. *Between* those six people, I prefer John for the job.
8. The job worked out *good.*
9. Your constant yelling *affects* my nerves.
10. The bridge is out; *precede* with caution.
11. "Me *to,*" she said.
12. Good *stationary* is difficult to buy these days.
13. The longest dictionaries are always those that are *abridged.*
14. *Raise* the roof if you must.
15. He bowed *respectively* before the queen.
16. He was the *latest* in many problems Mary faced.
17. She likes both sailboats and power boats, but he prefers the *latter.*
18. Be sure to *complement* your employees when they do a good job.
19. He *discovered* a new way to climb trees.
20. She traveled *farther* each day.
21. John requires much *counciling.*

ANSWERS

1. effects   2. correct   3. take   4. principal's   5. formerly
6. correct   7. Among   8. well   9. correct   10. proceed
11. too   12. stationery   13. unabridged   14. correct
15. respectfully   16. correct   17. correct   18. compliment
19. invented   20. correct   21. counseling

Problems with Spelling

Spelling plagues many writers. I remember one of my students, when I suggested he work on his spelling, saying, "Well, I try to come close." But spelling is one of the many activities in life where close doesn't count. A word is spelled either correctly or incorrectly. (There are a few exceptions where more than one spelling of a word is accepted.)

People with spelling problems, and that includes most of us to one degree or another, either misspell a word (writing *accomodate* instead of *accommodate,* for example) or confuse two words that sound alike, such as *it's* (the contraction) and *its* (the possessive form).

One way to overcome problems with spelling is to start a record of words that give you problems. Keep this record in your Writing Log on pages headed by letters of the alphabet and allow enough space for new entries. Write each word, divide it into syllables, and note the problem you have with it. Your list might appear as follows:

Spelling Record

Words	Syllables	Notes
accommodate	ac-com-mo-date	two *m*'s
accustomed	ac-cus-tomed	*o* after *t*, not *u*
analyze	an-a-lyze	*ze*, not *se*
appearance	ap-pear-ance	*ance*, not *ence*

Study the list of commonly misspelled words in Appendix 3. Then complete the following exercise.

EXERCISE

If the word is spelled correctly, write *correct.* If it is spelled incorrectly, write it correctly.

1.	interupt	13.	succede
2.	facinate	14.	decison
3.	equipped	15.	curriculum
4.	goverment	16.	incidently
5.	acustomed	17.	recomend
6.	existance	18.	privilege
7.	changable	19.	peice
8.	analysis	20.	misspelled
9.	analyse	21.	ocasion
10.	occured	22.	desireable
11.	niether	23.	benefitted
12.	truely	24.	desperate

ANSWERS

1. interrupt   2. fascinate   3. correct   4. government
5. accustomed   6. existence   7. changeable   8. correct
9. analyze   10. occurred   11. neither   12. truly   13. succeed
14. decision   15. correct   16. incidentally   17. recommend
18. correct   19. piece   20. correct   21. occasion
22. desirable   23. benefited   24. correct

Problems with Commas

Commas can help make writing easier to read and understand. But inappropriate use of commas or no use of commas can confuse the reader. Although the use of the comma is often a matter of judgment, there are certain instances where commas should be used. In general, use a comma—

• To separate independent clauses. A comma is used before a coordinating conjunction (*and, but, or,* etc.) connecting two clauses: "She drove to the village, but she wished she'd stayed home." In short sentences the comma is often dropped. Also, do not use a comma to splice groups of words together that could stand as independent sentences. It is incorrect to write, "She drove to the village, she wished she'd stayed home."

• To set off an introductory clause or a lengthy introductory phrase: "After practicing for months and making several attempts, Mary finally broke the jogging record." The comma is particularly important to set off phrases or clauses where words close together may be confused: "As the blacksmith pounded, every tourist in the shop watched him." "While Susan was eating, flies buzzed overhead." Without commas these sentences present a blacksmith pounding tourists and a woman eating flies. Do not use a comma after an introductory adverbial phrase that immediately precedes the verb it modifies: "From behind a boulder reared a massive Kodiak bear."

• To set off items in a series when there are three or more items: "Mary brought along bread, wine, cheese, and a big smile." If each of the items in the series is separated by a conjunction, commas should not be used: "Mary brought along bread and wine and cheese." If the items in the series contain internal commas, or the series is long and complex, separate the items with semicolons: "A carpenter needs at least the following for repairing a house: nails, screws, and bolts; paint, varnish, and shellac; and various kinds of wood."

• To set off a nonrestrictive phrase (a nonrestrictive phrase is one that can be left out of a sentence without affecting its meaning): "The jet plane, criticized by some, is quite an engineering marvel."

• To set off a nonrestrictive appositive (an appositive is an identifying phrase that is equivalent to the noun or pronoun it explains): "John, a salesman with the Ajax Company, comes well recommended."

• To set off names and other nouns directly addressed, whether occurring at the beginning, middle, or end of a sentence: "Sir, I disagree with your argument." "I believe, Mary, that you've gone too far this time." A missing comma in a direct address can change the meaning of a sentence dramatically. Compare "I remember, John" with "I remember John" or "Call me, Mary" with "Call me Mary."

• To separate two or more adjectives when each modifies the noun alone: "His shiny, black car ran over my lawn." No comma is needed if the first adjective modifies the idea presented by a combination of the second adjective and the noun: "He watched the angry storm clouds."

• To separate identical or similar words: "Given that, that is the way it will be."

• To separate titles, addresses, and dates: "Amos Johnson, club president, reported first." "She lives in Edmonton, Alberta." "On December 7, 1941, Japan attacked Pearl Harbor."

• To set off parenthetical elements that retain a close logical relationship to the remainder of the sentence: "Mason's review of the department was, to put it mildly, not well received."

• To set off interjections and similar elements that break the continuity of thought: "Oh, I didn't realize how concerned you'd be." "The idea, however, makes little sense."

Punctuating Quotations

Many writers have problems knowing when and where to place quotation marks and knowing when and where to place other punctuation when using quoted material.

Use quotation marks to set off the actual words of a speaker or writer. For example: The office manager said, "I want these reports finished by Thursday." When a quotation is interrupted by *she said, he asked,* etc., two sets of quotation marks are necessary. Example: "I refuse to accept your proposal," he said, "because you've not considered all the facts." Do not use quotation marks to set off an indirect quotation or paraphrase. Example: Mary said that she would not go along with the plan.

When a quotation is several paragraphs long, place opening quotation marks at the beginning of each paragraph to show that the quotation is continuing. Place closing quotation marks only at the end of the last paragraph of the quotation. When writing dialogue, a separate paragraph is usually allowed each speaker. You may also indicate a long quotation by introducing it with a colon and beginning the quotation on the next line, indenting it on both the left and the right. Because the indentation indicates a quotation, no quotation marks are necessary.

Use single quotation marks to indicate the inner quotation when you wish to show a quotation within a quotation. Example: John yelled, "Why does Susan always say, 'Do it over,' when she sees my work?"

Place periods and commas within quotation marks. Example: "The new computer is a marvel," said the sales rep.

Do not set off a quotation with commas when the quotation is the subject ("Seeing is believing" was the manager's slogan), the predicate nominative (The manager's slogan was "Seeing is believing"), or a restrictive appositive (The slogan "Seeing is believing" bothered many salespeople).

Place colons and semicolons outside quotation marks. Example: Beatrice said, "Only once will I do this"; then the door slammed shut.

Place exclamation points and question marks inside quotation marks only when they belong with the quoted matter. Examples: He asked, "Will I do it first?" Who once stated, "I only regret that I have but one life to lose for my country"? He shouted, "Shoot, shoot!" He whispered to me, "I'm leaving my wife"!

EXERCISES

Review several of your recent writing projects, looking for problems with the following:

1. plurals
2. perspectives (first person, second person, third person)
3. adjectives and adverbs (comparisons, adverbs with two forms, confusing adjectives and adverbs)
4. verbs (agreement between verbs and subjects, splitting infinitives)
5. possessives
6. agreement between pronouns and nouns
7. word usage (which words?)
8. spelling (which words?)
9. commas
10. quotations

In your Writing Log, note the problems you've discovered. Of the ten potential problem areas, which are most serious for you?

Chapter 9

Evaluating and Rewriting

The writing process is not complete when you roll the paper out of the typewriter for the first time. Many people may boast about completing a writing assignment the night before it was due and receiving a high grade from the professor or praise from their colleagues at work. However, in most cases, the writing would have been better if the author had allowed time for evaluating and rewriting.

When your writing first comes out of the typewriter, you usually see little fault with it. Your latest creation is undoubtedly the finest piece of writing you have ever done. That is only human nature, for much time, effort, and creative energy go into most writing projects. You feel good when you complete a piece of writing.

But set the writing aside for a few days and then pick it up again. What was once a flawless piece of writing has mysteriously developed a rash of errors, both small and large. Of course, the errors were there from the beginning, but in the excitement of completion you didn't see them.

Give your writing time to age. This aging period, minimally overnight, allows you to look again at what you have written with a more dispassionate and objective eye—akin to how your readers will view the material.

On the other hand, there are some writers who are so caught up with evaluating their writing that they write a sentence and then immediately begin to tinker with it, trying to improve it. Or they write a paragraph or two and then go back to rewrite, shifting words around and fussing over whether what they said on paper is what they had to say in their heads. For a few writers, this process works. For most writers, it doesn't. They become hopelessly bogged down in the details of the writing to the point where they may not even finish it. For most writers, the principle to follow is: Write all the way to the end before evaluating and rewriting.

Attitude Toward Evaluating and Rewriting

Before you can successfully evaluate and rewrite your own work, you must have a positive attitude toward the process. If you see it as drudgery and not nearly as important as other aspects of writing, you will have great difficulty doing it, and the results may be less than positive. Think of the photographer in the darkroom working on an enlargement and trying many different ways of cropping the negative before selecting the final enlargement and printing the picture. Or think of an architect designing a building. He or she has an idea of the building and begins sketching. Seldom is the first sketch accepted without modification. Sketches are discarded, modified, or combined until the idea is expressed in the best possible way.

Just as it is absurd for the photographer to accept the first attempt at cropping a negative or the architect to accept the first sketch of a building, it is absurd for you to believe a writing project is complete when the first draft is finished. You must come to see evaluating and rewriting as essential parts of a writing project, not something to be relegated to a last-minute effort to correct a few spelling errors and search for misplaced commas. The first draft is only the first major step in the completion of a writing project, not the end of the project. Evaluating and rewriting may often take as much time as creating the first draft.

Beginning writers (some advanced writers too) nurture and protect the words, paragraphs, and pages they've created. The thought of dropping not only words but entire paragraphs and sometimes whole pages can be shocking. Yet experienced writers know that evaluating and rewriting may result in cutting nearly half their pages. Although all writers feel protective toward what they have created, experienced writers nevertheless know that cutting out material, sometimes large chunks, is necessary for effective revisions.

Evaluating and rewriting entail (1) dropping or adding words, paragraphs, pages, even entire sections of a manuscript, (2) reorganizing sections within the manuscript, (3) starting fresh with certain aspects of the manuscript, and (4) sometimes starting all over again with an entirely new first draft.

Seeking criticism is an important step before rewriting. A critic may be an instructor in a course you are taking, a supervisor at work, an editor of a publication, or a reader invited by an editor to comment on your material. How do *you* react to such criticism, particularly if it sounds negative and suggests massive revisions of your creation?

One reaction is to become angry and defensive and vow that you'll do nothing to tamper with your creation. You know it's just right and your critic is either misinformed or not a careful reader of what you had to say. That is often the reaction of the inexperienced writer.

What is a more appropriate response? Let's look at an example. Suppose you have written an article and submitted it to a professional publication in your field. After a reasonable length of time, you receive copies of comments made by three reviewers from the editor of the publication. One reviewer suggests cutting the article by about one-third because it is too wordy. He gives specific examples of where he believes the cuts can be made. Another reviewer believes you used too few examples and asks for more. The third faults the structure of your article and offers suggestions for reorganizing the piece.

A reasonable response is to sort through the suggestions and accept those that will help improve the article. Even though you must develop an open attitude toward suggestions for revision, what you write is ultimately yours, and *you* must have the final say. Develop a balance between what you believe in and want to do and the suggestions that others make. Some writers try to incorporate all reviewer suggestions and then discover it is impossible because reviewers often contradict one another. It's only natural for different people to view a piece of writing in different ways. That is why it's useful to obtain more than one viewpoint on a piece of writing. But you must develop a positive attitude toward accepting such criticism. It's part of the process of evaluating and rewriting.

A Process for Evaluating and Rewriting

Three phases compose a process for evaluating and rewriting:

• Evaluating the meaning, tone, and rhythm of the writing

• Evaluating words, sentences, paragraphs, and the organization of the writing

• Correcting spelling, grammar, and punctuation

Caution: Don't attempt to complete all three evaluation phases with one reading. It's impossible to look for errors in tone, organization, and comma placement, for example, all in one reading.

Evaluating Meaning, Tone, and Rhythm

Once you've completed the rough draft of your writing assignment, read it all the way through, keeping in mind the following questions:

Do you have your audience clearly in mind? If you're writing an assignment for an instructor, that question is easily answered. But if you're writing a newsletter for your organization or an article for publication, the question may be more difficult. If you don't have your audience clearly in mind, you may find part of your manuscript highly technical and part of it written in a popular vein. The result would probably confuse both a technical and a broader audience.

Is the purpose for your writing clear? Are you writing to describe, narrate, explain, criticize, or persuade?

Is the tone what you want to convey? Is the tone appropriate for your audience and purpose? Is it plodding and heavy? Is it frivolous and insignificant? Is it arrogant and high-handed? Is it sincere, informal, hedging, vague, confused, or negative?

Does the material read smoothly? Does it "sound" right? Will it keep the reader reading?

EXERCISE

To assist with this first phase of evaluating and rewriting, it often helps to receive reaction from others. Ask a friend, your spouse, or a coworker to listen while you read aloud the first page or two of something you have recently written. Then ask the person these questions:

1. What do you remember from what I read?
2. How does the tone sound? How did it make you *feel?*
3. Which words do you remember that helped you grasp the meaning and purpose of the writing?
4. Which words do you remember that confused you or got in the way of understanding?
5. What do you believe is the purpose of the writing?

Evaluating Words, Sentences, Paragraphs, and the Organization of the Writing

Once you've worked through the first phase, you're ready to be more specific with your evaluation.

Evaluating Words

Some questions to answer when evaluating words:

Do you know what each word means and suggests? Can you eliminate some words without changing the meaning of your writing?

Have you always used the most precise word? Have you emphasized using first-degree words, avoiding the more complicated word when a simpler word means the same thing? Have you avoided jargon and pseudo-technical words?

Have you stressed the active voice?

Evaluating Sentences

Is each sentence necessary? Would the meaning of the writing change if the sentence were omitted? Would the writing be easier to understand if the sentence were omitted?

Does each sentence say exactly what you intended it to say?

Have you avoided misplaced phrases and modifiers?

Is the average sentence length short? (An average of eighteen to twenty words per sentence is a good goal.)

Have you varied the length of sentences? (Sentences of similar length make for boring reading.)

Evaluating Paragraphs

Is each paragraph necessary? Can some paragraphs be combined because they cover the same point? Should some paragraphs be divided because they cover several points?

Have you varied the length of paragraphs?

Does the first (lead) paragraph capture the reader's attention? give the reader an idea of what to expect? compel the reader to continue?

Does the closing paragraph tie the piece together? suggest future direction for the reader? avoid merely repeating what is in the piece?

Evaluating the Organization of the Writing

Is the organizational plan for the writing clear? Have you followed an organizational plan throughout, such as chronological order, space sequence, an inductive approach, a deductive approach, or a major topics approach?

Are transitions used to move the reader smoothly from main point to main point?

Are subheads used to help the reader understand the organization of the writing?

Correcting Spelling, Grammar, and Punctuation

Once you've completed the first two phases, you're ready to put the final touches on your writing. This final phase is exceedingly important, for it immediately gives your reader an overall impression of you as a writer. If your writing contains misspelled words, misplaced commas, and mutilated grammar, the reader immediately suspects the quality of your ideas and the care with which you researched and developed them. So it is time well spent to check carefully for problems with the details of your writing. Some questions to answer:

Have you checked the spelling of all words you're not sure of?

Have you checked punctuation for correctness and consistency throughout the writing? Have you checked punctuation to make certain it enhances rather than detracts from the meaning of the writing?

Have you checked capitalization for correctness and consistency?

Have you checked direct quotations to see that they are copied exactly?

EXERCISE

Using the three-step process outlined in this chapter, evaluate something you have written. Use the following checklist as a guide:

Evaluating Your Writing

A. Evaluating Meaning, Tone, and Rhythm

_____ Audience for writing is evident

_____ Purpose for writing is clear: to describe, narrate, explain, criticize, or persuade

_____ Material reads smoothly

_____ Tone is appropriate for audience and purpose

B. Evaluating Words, Sentences, Paragraphs, and Organization

_____ Excess words eliminated

_____ Precise words used

_____ Jargon and pseudo-technical words eliminated
_____ Active voice used
_____ Simpler words preferred to more complicated ones
_____ Each sentence necessary
_____ Misplaced phrases and modifiers eliminated
_____ Average length of sentences short
_____ Length of sentences varies
_____ Each paragraph necessary
_____ Each paragraph focuses on one idea
_____ Length of paragraphs varies
_____ Lead paragraph: captures attention, gives reader an idea of what to expect, compels reader to continue
_____ Closing paragraph: ties the writing together, suggests future direction for reader, avoids repeating
_____ Organizational plan for writing is clear: chronological order, space sequence, inductive approach, deductive approach, major topics approach, other
_____ Smooth transitions
_____ Subheads used to aid understanding

C. Correcting Spelling, Grammar, and Punctuation
_____ Words spelled correctly
_____ Consistent punctuation used throughout
_____ Punctuation enhances understanding
_____ Consistent capitalization used throughout
_____ Quotations copied correctly

Chapter 10

Taking Sexism
out of Writing

Whenever sexism in writing becomes the topic of discussion, someone will usually say, "What's the problem? Why are people so upset? We've had the English language for hundreds of years, and now we say it has a sexist flaw in it?"

Unfortunately, the English language *does* have a sexist flaw in it. And writers handle the problem in a variety of ways. Some ignore it, not recognizing or refusing to recognize that a problem exists. Fortunately, those writers who seek publication are constantly challenged by editors to rid their writing of its sexist tone.

Some writers, particularly book writers, include disclaimers in their introductions that say they know their writing may sound sexist but that the flaw is in the English language. Then they go on writing as if no problem existed.

Other writers try to solve the problem by alternating *she, hers,* and *her* with *he, his,* and *him.* And still others try to solve the pronoun problem with cute little adaptations such as *s/he* or *he/she.*

Many writers, though, solve the sexist writing problem in a way that doesn't destroy the tone and rhythm of their writing. It is this last approach that will be discussed in this chapter.

Problems with Third-Person Pronouns and the Generic *Man*

Unfortunately, English does not have third-person pronouns that are neutral. *He, his,* and *him* are *not* neutral, though some people still claim they may be used that way. We still see such statements as "The employee will be disciplined if he is consistently late for work." The intent of the statement is that both men and women employees will be disciplined.

There are also problems with the supposedly "generic" *man:* "All of *mankind* will suffer." "Down through the ages, *man* has survived adversity." *Mankind* and *man* in these two sentences are intended to refer to both men and women.

So what's the problem if we can agree that the personal pronouns *he, his,* and *him* and the word *man* can be used to mean both men and women? Are we creating a problem when one doesn't exist to appease a small number of people? No, the problem *does* exist, and it is a serious one from at least two perspectives: being fair to both men and women and presenting clear writing to readers.

First, you must convey in your writing a clear sense of equality and personal worth of men and women. When you use the so-called neutral personal pronouns *he, his,* and *him* and the generic *man,* you often communicate an unintended message that goes well beyond the writing itself. You are saying to your reader that you are not sensitive to the issues that are inherent in their use.

Second, people are often confused when words like *he* and *man* are used to mean sometimes men and sometimes both sexes. For instance, in the following quotation, do *himself* and *he* refer to both men and women or to men alone?

> Consider, firstly, two comparatively simple situations in which a cyberneticist might find himself. He has a servomechanism, or a computing machine, with no randomizing element, and he also has a wife.[1]

Until you arrive at the very end of the quotation, you can go along with the generic *he,* but at the end you clearly know the writer is talking about a man.

The use of the generic *man* also presents some interesting problems when the situation is examined more closely. Janice Moulton suggests a look at this classic syllogism:

> All men are mortal.
> Socrates is a man.
> Socrates is mortal.

So far so good. We've all read it before and believe we understand what it means. The word *men* in the first line is clearly used in a generic sense. But Moulton then offers the following adaptation for consideration:

All men are mortal.
Sophia is a man.
Sophia is mortal.

If Sophia is a woman, we have some definite problems with the second line.

Moulton makes clear that for a word to be gender neutral you must be able to use it with women as well as with men. Most agree that the word *human* is gender neutral. You can thus write, "Some humans are women," and have an acceptable statement. But if you insist that the word *man* is as neutral as *human,* you need only test it with the following: "Some men are women."

Given the problems with third-person pronouns and the generic *man,* what are the alternatives?

Consider the following statement: "The employee is not aware of his responsibilities." How could you rewrite the sentence to overcome the sexist problem?

You could write, "The employee is not aware of his or her responsibilities." You're on the way. You're aware of the problem and want to make certain the reader knows that the message is for both men and women employees. But as you will see below, there are alternatives that should be used unless you have no other choice. Repeated use of *he or she* and *his or her* stifles the flow of writing and calls attention to your concern with sexism. Even worse is using such gimmicks as *he/she, his/her,* and *s/he.*

Another way to handle the problem is to change *employee* to its plural form and write, "Employees are not aware of their responsibilities." That allows you to use the plural and gender-neutral pronoun *their.* Never, never use the plural *their* with a singular antecedent. It is not grammatically correct to write, "The employee is not aware of their responsibilities."

Sometimes writing in the second person avoids the problem entirely: "You may not be aware of your responsibilities." Second-person writing has other advantages as well—it is often warmer and more personal.

What do you do about the problem of the generic *man?* Consider the following:

Sexist Form	**Possible Substitutions**
Man is a social animal.	People are social animals.
since the beginning of mankind	since the beginning of civilization
man's achievements	human achievements
best man for the job	best person for the job
grow to manhood	grow to adulthood
primitive man	primitive people, primitive human beings

EXERCISE

Rewrite the following sentence in as many ways as you can to eliminate the sexism but retain the meaning:
"Each person writes his own report."

POSSIBLE SOLUTIONS

1. People write their own reports.
2. You will write your own report. (if this form fits the situation)
3. Each person writes an individual report. (Sometimes the pronoun can be changed to another word.)
4. Each person writes his or her own report.
5. A report is written by each person. (This is the least preferred because it is in the passive voice and thus weak.)

EXERCISE

Rewrite the following sentences to correct the problem of the generic *man.*

1. In the end, man will survive.
2. John was studying the history of man.
3. What does it take to make a man?
4. Poets are the first instructors of mankind.

POSSIBLE SOLUTIONS

1. In the end, humans will survive.
2. John was studying the history of civilization.
3. What does it take to make a person?
4. Poets are the first instructors of the human race.

Problems with Job Titles

Although many women will continue to hold such traditional jobs as secretary, nurse, and homemaker, you must avoid suggesting those as the only jobs for women.[2] And you must recognize that many men serve as secretaries, nurses, and homemakers as well. Because both women and men work as doctors, lawyers, bricklayers, professors, social workers, and gardeners, you should remove from your writing such terms as *lady lawyer, woman doctor, male nurse,* and *male secretary.* Such terms as *poetess* and *authoress* are taboo. Other common occupational terms ending in *-man* can be corrected as follows:

Inappropriate Version	Corrected Version
foreman	supervisor
insurance man	insurance agent
congressman	representative
fireman	fire fighter
policeman	police officer
mailman	mail carrier
cameraman	camera operator
businessman	business person, business manager
salesman	salesperson, clerk

The word *chairman* gives people more grief than most. Some people have made a strong case that it must be used in its traditional form. Others have developed a number of alternative forms, such as *chair, chairperson, chairman* (when referring to a man), *chairwoman* (when referring to a woman), *presiding officer, head, leader, moderator,* and *committee head.* (*Chairperson* is rather commonly used these days.)

Along with the obvious problem of job titles is the more subtle problem of life-styles for women and men. When you use the term *career women,* you are calling attention to women who pursue a career as unusual, when in fact they are not unusual at all. You would never use *career men.* Using *career women* to refer to those who pursue a career outside the home is also an affront to those women who see their career, at least at one stage of their lives, as caring for their children at home.

Human Terms

Besides avoiding job stereotyping, you must also avoid stereotyping the sexes. Traditionally men have been praised for their strength, assertiveness, boldness, and initiative. Women, on the other hand, have been recognized for their compassion, sensitivity, and gentleness. Men are viewed as logical and decisive, women as intuitive and scatterbrained. Men face decisions with rationality, women with emotion. Clearly, both men and women share all these qualities, and your writing should reflect this.

Descriptions of Men and Women

Both sexes should be described in similar terms. It is inappropriate to write, "John Moore is a highly competent lawyer, and his wife, Jane, is a beautiful brunette." More accurately you could write, "The Moores are an attractive couple. John is a handsome blond, and Jane is a beautiful brunette." Or "The Moores are highly respected in their fields. Jane is an accomplished artist, and John is a successful lawyer." Or, if more appropriate, you could write, "The Moores are an interesting couple. John is a successful lawyer, and Jane is active in community and church affairs."

Also, avoid using phrases that stereotype women, such as *scatterbrained woman, frustrated spinster, the fair sex, the weaker sex, the little woman,* and *sweet young thing.* Do not use *girl,* as in, "I'll have my girl find the report for you." Instead write, "I'll have my secretary [or assistant] find the report for you." Or better still, "I'll have Jane [or John] find the report for you." Do not use *girls* or *ladies* when you are referring to adult females; use *women.*

Many women who work in the home do not want to be called housewives. (When I slip and use the word, my wife reminds me that she is not married to a house.) Use *homemaker* for a person who works at home, or use another appropriate term that is more specific. For example, do not write, "Housewives are feeling the pinch of higher meat prices." Instead write, "Consumers [or shoppers] are feeling the pinch of higher meat prices."

Just as women should not be stereotyped in your writing, neither should men. Avoid suggesting that men are dependent on women to cook their meals and that they are clumsy when doing chores around the house. In an office setting, avoid suggesting that men are hopelessly lost when trying to find something in the file or grossly inept at operating office equipment efficiently.

Women as Participants in the Action

In some traditional writing, women are portrayed as possessions of men and not as equal participants in the action. For instance: "The settlers moved to the Midwest, taking their wives and children with them." An alternative would be "Settler families moved into the Midwest."

Also, women should not be portrayed as requiring permission from their husbands to do something, as in, "John allows his wife to bowl on Wednesday evenings," or "Jim permits Mary to work part-time."

Parallel Treatment

The English language has such a long history of unequal treatment of men and women that it is sometimes difficult to spot such problems as nonparallel treatment. *Man and wife* and *men and ladies* are nonparallel. The correct parallel forms are *husband and wife, men and women,* and *ladies and gentlemen.*

It is not appropriate to refer to a man and a woman by using only his last name but both of her names, as in, "Smith and Jane Johnson will attend the meeting." Instead write, "Smith and Johnson . . ." or "John and Jane . . ."

Unnecessary reference to a woman's marital status should also be avoided. Increasingly, many women prefer the title *Ms.* rather than *Miss* or *Mrs. Mr.* has no marital designation, and many women want to be considered in like fashion. *Ms.* is also a very useful form of address when you don't know a woman's marital status.

EXERCISES

1. In your Writing Log, write your feelings about sexism in writing.
2. Examine at least three pieces of writing you've done recently

and note the sentences in which you used *he, his,* or *him* to refer to both sexes. Write each sentence in at least two other ways, avoiding sexism.
3. Using the same pieces of writing, note where you've used *man* to mean both men and women. What alternative forms could you have used?

NOTES

1. L. Jonathan Cohen, "Can There Be Artificial Minds?" *Reason and Responsibility,* 2nd ed., Joel Feinberg, ed. (Encino, Calif.: Dickenson Publishing Company, 1971), p. 288, quoted by Janice Moulton in "The Myth of the Neutral 'Man'," Mary Vetterling-Braggin, Frederick A. Elliston, and Jane English, *Feminism and Philosophy* (Totowa, N.J.: Littlefield, Adams and Company, 1977).
2. Ideas for this and following sections were adapted in part from *Guidelines for Equal Treatment of the Sexes in McGraw-Hill Book Company Publications* (New York: McGraw-Hill).

Chapter 11

Writing for Educational Assignments

If you are a student and have writing assignments as a part of your educational responsibilities, this chapter is for you. You'll probably be asked to write term papers, laboratory reports, book reports, essay examinations, and perhaps a graduate research proposal and a thesis or dissertation. The following are those writing problems that occur most often when students write:

• Starting too late on a major writing project. Many students wait until the last few weeks of a semester to begin a major term paper for a course. Not surprisingly, they run into problems varying from finding reference material to having no time at all for rewriting and polishing their papers. College students speak of "pulling all-nighters"—cramming for an exam or writing a term paper to be turned in the following morning. All-night term paper writing (panic deadline writing, I call it) still occurs all too often. And nineteen-year-old freshmen are not the only guilty ones. Forty-year-old graduate students try to do the same thing. In nearly every instance, such panic deadline writing is a disaster. A few students who have a particular talent, an extraordinary supply of reference materials, or a lot of luck may be able to work this way, but don't *you* count on it.

• A topic that is too broad. Whether the writing assignment is a term paper or a dissertation, nearly every student has a problem developing a manageable topic. When beginning a writing assignment, the tendency is to panic a little and wonder how you can ever find enough information to write about. You decide to solve the problem by keeping your topic broad. But when you begin to dig into the reference materials, you almost always discover the topic is more extensive than you imagined. If you continue with it, you soon are hopelessly lost in a heap of notecards and reference books. Unless you retreat to a narrower, more carefully defined topic, your final paper is either a superficial discourse or a needlessly long paper.

• Fear of putting oneself into the writing. Somewhere on college campuses must exist a little book that says students should never put themselves into their writing but rather include quotation after quotation. Unfortunately, that's how much student writing appears. Footnotes are stacked up at the bottoms of pages, and quotations are interrupted only with occasional attempts at transition.

This mysterious little guidebook must expound a rule that says the following: Once on a college campus, students must deny all their experiences, repress all their feelings, and dig for what an authority has said on the topic. That is, of course, pure nonsense, particularly for returning students who have a wealth of personal experience to share on many topics.

• Reluctance to rewrite material. You've probably heard a friend say, "When it comes out of my typewriter, it's done. I don't have time for any of this rewriting business." Many students *don't* have time because they are panic deadline writers. And many students who have time don't take it because they don't see the value of rewriting.

• A belief that it's the content that counts, not how it's written. Content and presentation cannot be separated. What is written and how it is written go hand in hand. Something said poorly is as much a failure as having nothing to say.

• Little attention to the mechanics of writing. Too many student writers turn in papers with misspelled words, bad grammar, and misplaced punctuation. Such sloppy attention to writing mechanics detracts from what they're trying to say, though they often argue that it shouldn't. If a student hasn't been careful with writing details such as spelling, grammar, and correct punctuation, what assurance does the instructor have that this student has been careful with the content?

• A mistaken idea about academic writing style. It seems that mysterious little book must also include a rule stated thus: A term paper, a dissertation, or a report should be dull, wordy, and incomprehensible.

Samuel Williamson must have found that little book and quoted from it when he wrote, with tongue in cheek:

Rule 1. Never use a short word when you can think of a long one.
Rule 2. Never use one word when you can use two or more.
Rule 3. Put one-syllable thought into polysyllabic terms.
Rule 4. Put the obvious in terms of the unintelligible.
Rule 5. Announce what you are going to say before you say it.
Rule 6. Defend your style as "scientific."[1]

• Too much concern with "what the instructor wants." Of course, most educational writing is written for instructors who have the responsibility for reading it and assigning a grade. It's only natural that you should be concerned with what your instructor prefers in writing assignments. Unfortunately, some students spend more time reading their instructor's writing, talking with their instructor's former students, and generally trying to "figure out" their instructor than they do planning, researching, and writing their papers.

Writing a Term Paper

A term paper is a documented piece of writing that explores a topic in depth. It is a lesser treatment than a thesis or a dissertation but deeper than a book report or a laboratory report. Following is a procedure for term paper writing. However, the entire process of term paper writing is dynamic. Although it is presented here as a series of consecutive steps, you may arrive at one step only to discover you must go back to a previous one.

1. Select a topic. Your instructor may assign a broad topic area and give you the responsibility of deciding what you want to write about within that area and with the course objectives in mind. (This seems to be the most common form of term paper assignment.) Or your instructor may allow you full responsibility for selecting your topic. In either case, select a topic that interests you. You'll spend hours thinking about, researching, and writing about your topic. If the topic doesn't interest you, the writing process will become increasingly difficult.

Select a topic that will help your understanding of the coursework. If you're a graduate student, select a topic that will help you obtain some insight into possible future thesis or dissertation topics.

Be sure information is available for the topic you select. Ask the reference librarian whether information on your topic is available in your library or through interlibrary loan. If your topic requires interviewing experts, check to see whether this will be possible.

Select a topic that will allow you to complete your term paper during the semester or quarter in which the class meets. A term paper carried over into another semester or vacation period can lose your interest rapidly and become a burden as you continue other courses. A key to finishing a term paper within the time limits of a course is to begin the project toward the beginning rather than the end of the course. If you're taking a typical sixteen-week course, select a term paper topic about the sixth week. Too often students wait until the twelfth or even the fourteenth week and find that they don't have enough time to complete satisfactory term papers.

Be sure your topic is neither too broad nor too narrow. Students often have problems narrowing a topic to a manageable size. Some students go too far and select such a narrow topic that their work has little meaning. Of course, judgment is involved in knowing when a topic is too broad or too narrow.

Suppose you're in a geology course and can choose your own term paper topic within the overall course objectives. You decide to write a paper on the geology of Wisconsin. After an hour or so of research, you realize that the geology of Wisconsin is far too broad a topic. So you select glacial effects on Wisconsin. With some further reading on upper midwestern glaciers, you discover that your topic is still too broad. You decide to pursue terminal moraines. When you begin reading about terminal moraines, you discover their characteristics, where they are located, why they appear as they do today. You decide it would be interesting to write about the terminal moraine in central Wisconsin. And after focusing on the terminal moraine in central Wisconsin, you run across some information about the terminal moraine in western Waushara County.

At what point in this process of topic selection was the topic too broad, and when was it too narrow? The topics again, from broad to narrow, are (1) the geology of Wisconsin, (2) glacial effects on

Wisconsin, (3) terminal moraines, (4) the terminal moraine in central Wisconsin, and (5) the terminal moraine in western Waushara County. Certainly topics 1 and 2 are too broad. Topic 3 may be about right for a term paper. If you are able to find the information and are so inclined, topic 4 may also be a good term paper topic. It's specific, yet it covers enough geographic area to give you considerable room for developing the topic. Topic 5 is too narrow for a term paper. It is better suited as a topic for a research report.

2. Decide on the purpose. A term paper, like other writing, may have a variety of purposes. Remember that the purpose of writing may be to *describe* something or someone; to *narrate*, or report the incidents about an event; to *explain* a situation, a process, or a viewpoint; to *criticize* something or someone; or to *persuade* someone they should do something or accept a particular point of view or conclusion.

Let's take the example of the topic of the terminal moraine in central Wisconsin. How might you focus that topic to accomplish different purposes?

You could *describe* the terminal moraine in central Wisconsin, where it is located, how it appears today, its effects on agriculture in the area, and so on.

You could *narrate* a step-by-step account of the movement of the glacier, its decline, and the formation of the terminal moraine.

You could discuss the various theories that *explain* the process by which the terminal moraine developed.

You could discuss the various theories about the formation of the terminal moraine, showing the strengths and weaknesses of each, and then *criticize* each of the theories.

You could try to *persuade* your reader to accept one of the terminal moraine theories.

Too often students don't decide on a purpose for their term papers, or they unknowingly combine several purposes. When a paper is a combination of several purposes, it often has none.

3. Develop questions to guide your research. Your questions are, of course, influenced by the purpose for your paper. Using the example of the terminal moraine, some initial questions might be, What is a terminal moraine? What caused it? What are its components? When did terminal moraines appear? Why did they occur? Where are they found? How do they affect people today?

Jot down as many questions as you can. As you begin

researching, you'll add many more questions to your list. With the list of questions, you're ready for step 4.

4.   Research the topic. This will likely be the most time consuming of all the steps in term paper writing. Chapter 3 includes detailed information about researching. Some practical tips that are often overlooked:

Take time to write legibly.

Copy direct quotations accurately. Find original sources when you can. If the source you found is quoting another source, go directly to the source quoted. And go beyond written materials when possible: write or call the experts on a topic.

Make certain every research note has either a footnote or a complete bibliographic entry (see Appendix 4) written at the time you write the note. Nothing wastes more time than going back to find a publisher's name, a date, etc. But keep a record of library call numbers just in case you have to find a book a second time.

Maintain a skeptical attitude. Always look for more than one perspective on a topic.

5.   Begin to outline your paper. That doesn't necessarily limit you to the formal outlining procedure that you may have learned back in high school. If you find that system of outlining useful, use it. If not, you may prefer instead to begin writing the term paper and then organize the material during the revision. It doesn't matter whether you begin with an outline or work on an outline as you begin writing. Somewhere in the process you must organize your ideas.

During the outlining phase be conscious of your purpose (what organizational approach will help meet the purpose?), the topic itself (does one organizational approach work better than another for this topic?), and your own writing and research approach (does it work better for you to organize and then write or to write and then organize?).

6.   Write the first draft. Remember that a term paper, like other writing, has a beginning, a middle, and an ending. The beginning introduces your topic and gets your reader into it. The middle develops the topic according to your purpose, and the ending ties it together.

7.   Set the writing aside and evaluate. This is an extremely important step in the writing process and one that is most often violated by student writers. They don't plan well enough to allow time to leave the writing for a while and then come back and rewrite. Without the time, no one can do a thorough job of evaluating and rewriting.

8.   Rewrite. Once you've finished evaluating, rewrite your term paper. Then it's back to more evaluating and the possibility of further rewriting. Even though evaluating and rewriting are extremely important in producing quality term papers, students most often overlook these steps or consider them only superficially.

Writing a Laboratory Report

A lab report is written after you conduct an experiment as part of a laboratory course, observe a demonstration, or return from a field trip. Generally, a lab report comprises the following: (1) an abstract, (2) an introduction, (3) a methods section explaining how the experiment or demonstration was carried out, (4) a results section explaining what was found out, (5) a discussion of the results and suggestions for further research.

When writing the report, be sure to define terms carefully, use examples to support main points, and present accurate and complete information. Write in a logical sequence and state conclusions that are reasonable given the evidence presented.

Writing a Book Report

A book report should not be confused with a book review (see chapter 13 for a discussion of how to write book reviews). A book review is a careful analysis of a book, with comments about completeness, accuracy, and style of writing; the book report merely tells its readers what the book is about. No attempt is made to analyze or judge the content or the quality of the presentation. In common with a book review, a book report begins with a complete bibliographic entry. This includes the author's name, city of publication, publisher, and copyright date.

After giving such information, go on to report briefly what the book is about. Some instructors ask that a book report be no longer than a couple of paragraphs; others ask that you write five or more double-spaced typewritten pages about a book. Often a book report is slanted toward the content of a particular course. You are asked to report on a book or several books from the perspective of their relationship to the content of the course.

At no time during a book report do you make judgments about the quality of the book. The book report is a report, and that's all. It tells the reader what a book is about.

Writing an Essay Examination

Nearly all students, young and old, fear examinations. They wonder, Will I be able to do it? Will my mind go blank when I sit down and face the examination? What will my instructor and what will my family think of me if I fail? Will I be able to control my emotions and not allow the butterflies in my stomach to take over once I begin writing the exam? Have I studied the right material? The list of anxiety questions that builds in the minds of students is a long one. Here are some tips to help you overcome test anxiety and succeed on essay examinations.

Before the Examination

1. Keep up with reading and general class assignments. Keep up-to-date and legible lecture notes. Review your progress in understanding the content of the course starting with the very first week. Frame questions for yourself about the content and then write answers to them. Work with a friend who is also taking the course and ask questions of each other. Do this at least weekly, if possible.

2. Try to see the "big picture" for the course. How do the various pieces that you are studying day to day mesh into a larger whole? How do the various pieces you are studying relate to the overall course objectives?

3. Determine how the required readings and other out-of-class assignments relate to what is covered during class. How do the content of the readings and the content of the lectures either add to each other or provide new areas of information for you?

4. Find out what kind of essay examinations your instructor gives. Ask him or her whether examples of examinations are available for inspection. Ask former students about the examinations your instructor gives. Sometimes examination files are available for courses; check to see whether they are available for your course.

5. Avoid cramming prior to examinations. Systematic, long-term study will provide a much broader and deeper basis for examination than a couple of all-night cramming sessions. Do review before the test, but don't depend on what you do the last few days before the examination to carry you through.

During the Examination

1. Arrive early so you can find the examination room easily and have a few minutes to catch your breath and relax before the examination begins.

2. When you are handed the examination, read the instructions carefully. Also jot down any oral instructions your instructor may give you. Pay particular attention to the following key words that are clues to the kind of answer you should write:

Define. Write in a clear, concise way the meaning of what you are asked to define. Show what clearly differentiates what you are defining from everything else.

Explain. Show the how and the why of what you are asked to explain. If you can, state the causes.

Analyze. Indicate the parts of what you are asked to analyze and show the relationship of the parts to one another and to the whole.

List. In tabular form, itemize your answer to the question. Complete sentences may not be necessary.

Compare. Show how the items you are asked to compare are both similar and different.

Contrast. Show how the items you are asked to contrast differ from each other. Do not indicate how they are similar.

Outline. With short phrases, indicate the main points and important supporting information. Do not write complete sentences unless specifically asked to.

Let's take the example of the Wisconsin glacier mentioned earlier in this chapter. Here are a series of example essay examination questions showing the application of the above key words.

Define the terminal moraine.

Explain the effects of the glacier on Wisconsin.

Analyze the effects of the glacier on Wisconsin.

List the characteristics of the driftless area.

Compare the driftless area with the glaciated area.

Contrast the driftless area with the glaciated area.

Outline the effects of the glacier on Wisconsin.

3. When you begin the examination, answer those questions that you believe you know best.

4. Answer the questions as completely as you can, but don't give information that is not asked for. The clutter of unrelated information may draw attention from your answer. If the question asks you to define something, don't go on and do an analysis.

5. Before writing the answer to a question, develop a brief outline of your answer on a scrap piece of paper. This allows you to think through your answer and prevents you from writing quickly and then discovering that you've omitted an important part of your answer.

6. Unless you are specifically asked not to, write your responses in complete sentences.

7. Leave space at the end of each answer in case you think of additional information that is important and relevant.

8. Write legibly. If your instructor has to guess at your writing, you may not receive the benefit of the doubt.

9. Read each answer to correct spelling errors, punctuation, grammar, and any obvious word omissions. Also read the answer to make sure you've really answered the question.

10. If you discover you are out of time with questions remaining to be answered, outline the answers rather than leave them blank. You'll likely receive partial credit for your efforts.

After the Examination

Try not to write the examination over and over again in your mind as you wait for the results. Work on another course or another class project until you receive your examination back.

When you receive your corrected examination, study your instructor's comments carefully. If there is a comment you don't understand, make an appointment and talk with him or her. Don't approach your instructor, though, with the idea that you want to have your grade changed. That seldom works. But do point out to an instructor if he or she has erred in adding up points, missed reading part of your answer on the back of a page, and so on. Instructors are cool toward students who routinely try to raise their examination scores. On the other hand, most instructors are quite happy to discuss an examination with a student, showing where the student has misunderstood a question, answered incompletely, and so on.

Once you have your corrected examination, go back to your lecture notes, textbooks, and other reference materials to find the answers that you missed. An examination can be an excellent learning device if you allow it to be. Examinations do not have the sole purpose of screening out the competent from the incompetent, as some students imagine.

Writing a Thesis or a Dissertation

Theses and dissertations are original reports of research, much longer and more comprehensive than the laboratory report discussed earlier in this chapter. Some undergraduate students are required to write senior theses; many master's degree students are required to write graduate theses; and every doctoral student who works on a Ph.D. is required to write a dissertation.

The form of the thesis or dissertation varies, depending on whether a student is majoring in a science field like botany, in a humanities field like history, or in a social science field like sociology. But there are some common elements too. In nearly every instance, the student is required to submit a proposal for the research prior to actually conducting the research and writing the thesis or dissertation.

Prior to writing a research proposal, you should answer several questions:

Is this a research topic for which you have a deep and intense interest? Because research takes considerable time and often money, you should be highly interested in the topic. The project, from the beginning of the proposal to the completion of the thesis or dissertation, may take two, three, or more years to complete. Occasionally students tire of their research halfway through the project, when it is often too late to turn back. The remaining time on the project is sheer agony for both student and professor and sometimes results in an unfinished graduate program.

Is your research interest within the competency and interest of your major or research professor? If not, you may be in for trouble. Your major professor may not be able to provide you with the assistance you need and the support you require.

Have you selected a topic that can be researched in a reasonable amount of time? Have you selected a topic that will allow you to collect the data and other information you need in a year or so, so that you can complete your thesis or dissertation in a reasonable amount of time? Sometimes you do not know how long it will take to research a topic until you begin researching it. If this is the case, you may want to begin some of your research before you complete your proposal. That will give you a better idea of how long it will take to finish the research. An alternative is to write a proposal indicating that during the first phase of the research, you wish to explore the topic and discuss what it consists of, how broad or narrow it is, what the questions are, and so on.

Do you have the resources necessary to do your research? If you are planning a mail or telephone survey, are you aware of the costs involved? If you plan to interview people, do you know the travel costs? If your project involves the use of a computer, do you have an estimate of the costs? Will you personally type the final copy of your research paper or hire a typist? Typing can cost one dollar a page or more. Total financial costs for a research project should be planned from beginning to end, just as the content of the research is planned.

Does your major professor have a research grant and a project that you can work on within that grant? That is, of course, an ideal situation. You are usually paid as a research assistant, you have the costs of data collection and analysis paid for by the project, and you have a close working relationship with a professor who is eager to see the entire research project succeed, including your part of it. The problem is to make certain the research project offered to you by a professor is compatible with your interests. Working on a professor's research project has many advantages, but if you are not completely interested in the project, you will spend several dreary years.

The Proposal

Although it varies from department to department and from discipline to discipline, a research proposal generally includes the following components:

• An introduction, or brief statement of what the research is about, the questions to be answered, and the overall purposes of the research.

• A background statement, which presents the context for the research. This could include a discussion of the theory or theories out of which the research has originated. It could also include the historical context of the research, the social context, and whatever other information helps provide the reader with a sense of where the research fits.

• The research problem or question, a brief statement that says clearly what question or questions the student hopes to answer with the research. Many students have problems writing a clear, well-thought-out research problem. It is worth spending time writing the research problem because it is key to the entire research project. All the other components of the research relate to the research problem.

• A review of the literature and possibly a theoretical framework. In this section a review of other research on the topic is presented. Also, the theory out of which the research originates or the theory to which the research relates may be explained in considerable detail. Not all research has a theoretical framework, but all research has some related research to be reported. This section says to your reader that you've examined the research area to the extent that you know what others have done and what they have found out. This section also helps your reader know where your research fits within what has been done—how it helps add to a body of knowledge about a topic.

• The objective and/or hypothesis of the study. An objective is a statement that indicates what you hope to accomplish in your research. A hypothesis is a statement that you attempt to refute in your research. For instance, a hypothesis may be written: "There is no relationship between the number of hours a student studies for an examination and the grade received."

All research proposals will have statements of objectives, but not all will include a statement of a hypothesis. Refer to research methods books for more information about the purpose and approaches for writing hypotheses (see chapter 14 for a list of these references).

• Research methods. This section includes a description of your plans for conducting the research. For instance, you may plan to develop a survey instrument and mail it, or to interview people, or perhaps to do library research using historical data. Whatever the source of your research information, indicate what it is and how you plan to obtain the information. Sometimes it helps to develop a timetable of when you plan to accomplish various tasks. For instance, your timetable may say: May–July, develop and test survey form; August–November, mail surveys; December–March, code data for computer application; and so on. If you plan to do a statistical analysis of your data, state which statistical tests you plan to use.

• The significance of the research, stating the importance of your research and what contribution it will make to solving some practical problem, further developing some theory, or adding to a body of knowledge in your field.

• Definitions of terms. If your research includes unfamiliar terms, provide a section in the proposal where you define them.

• A bibliography listing the writings that relate to your research topic. You will discuss many of them in the review of literature section.

The Thesis or Dissertation

Although you may think so after reading other theses and dissertations, there is no required writing style. Unfortunately, many students and their professors believe that theses and dissertations should be unnecessarily obscure in their presentation. Thus, theses and dissertations have reputations for being the most difficult of all writing to read and understand. That does not need to be. All the ideas discussed so far in this book apply to thesis and dissertation writing just as much as they do to any other kind of serious nonfiction writing. Because you are often working with technical matters such as statistical tests, hypothesis testing, and the like, you are challenged to write in such a way that your readers can understand you.

Perhaps you have heard that only your major professor and other members of your graduate committee will read your thesis or dissertation. Sometimes that is the case. But if you have researched an important area, others will read the material as well. What kind of impression do you wish to leave?

Besides the problem of obscure writing, graduate student researchers often face a number of other problems that have already been discussed:

• Writer's block. Often a student researcher collects boxes full of information for a research project and then finds that the job of writing words on a piece of paper is an overwhelming task. Some graduate student researchers put off their writing for weeks, which eventually become months and then years. Soon they are so far from their projects that the projects have become impossible to complete. Others are so overwhelmed with all the information they've collected that they just don't know where to begin writing, so they don't begin at all.

• Structuring. Figuring out how to organize your thesis or dissertation can save you hours of time. It can also help you overcome writer's block caused by not knowing where to start writing.

• Discipline and time planning. A thesis or dissertation is considerably different from a term paper, a laboratory or book report, an essay examination, or any other writing assignment you may have faced as a student. It simply cannot be written in one sitting. Thus, you must plan your time so you can work on your thesis or dissertation every day. One technique is to give yourself a writing goal, say five pages a day. No matter what, write at least five pages every day. If you work on your project five days a week, that adds up to twenty-five pages of manuscript. And if you work twenty days a month, you then have one hundred pages after a month's work. Thinking about your thesis or dissertation in terms of what you can accomplish in a day is easier than thinking about the entire project, which may be three hundred or more pages.

NOTES

1. Samuel T. Williamson, "How to Write like a Social Scientist," in Norman Cousins, ed., *Writing for Love or Money* (New York: Longmans, Green and Co., 1949), pp. 196–202.

Chapter 12

Writing for Professional Requirements

Subscribers to the *Harvard Business Review* rated the ability to communicate as the prime requisite of a promotable executive. Interestingly, the ability to communicate was rated over such characteristics as ambition and drive, college education, ability to make sound decisions, self-confidence, good appearance, and the ability to get things done with and through people.[1]

Many of the writing problems already discussed in this book apply to professionals: researching, organizing to write, writing for different purposes, knowing the mechanics, sexism in writing, and readability. The emphasis in this chapter will be on specific writing requirements: memos, newsletters, reports, and proposals—requirements that many professionals face in their day-to-day work.

Writing a Memo

At one time or another, you've probably read a memo and then had to phone the writer to ask what the memo was about. You've probably written memos like that too. I know I have.

Let's say you plan to miss a staff meeting and want to inform your supervisor. Your memo might read:

June 18

Jane:

Sorry I can't attend next Wednesday's staff meeting. I'll be in Chicago.

Paul

Clear, concise, and to the point—enough to communicate the message. Short memos usually aren't problems. It's the longer ones that cause trouble. A longer memo should include (1) the date, (2) the name(s) of the recipient(s), (3) the name of the sender, (4) a short summary of content, and (5) the names of people to receive copies. For example, the format for a longer memo might appear as follows:

July 21

To: Mary James

From: J. W. Anderson

Subject: A recommendation to study the complaints about
        the mailing department

(Content of memo)

cc: Fred Johnson, Laurie Smyth

Memos are written for a variety of purposes, including to inform, to ask for a decision, to make an inquiry, to respond to an inquiry, to call for action, and to express thanks.

The first step in writing a memo is to decide the purpose(s) of the memo. Know exactly what you wish to communicate: the results of a meeting you attended, what you observed when you visited an office, a request for a new piece of equipment for your department, or a thank-you to a coworker who helped you with a difficult assignment.

The second step is to say what you have to say in a minimum number of words. Ask yourself, What are the three or four main points I want to include? You might find it helpful to jot down your main points in outline fashion. In that way you'll be guided toward sticking to the essentials yet covering what you want to cover in the memo. Write the three or four main points and then quit.

For example, a memo asking for information might appear thus:

July 12

To: Frank Lufler
        George Lovell
        Alice Lodge

From: J. W. Anderson

Subject: Request for research reports

I'm writing our year-end report of research accomplishments for our department. Would you send me the following information before August 15:

1. The names of the staff members who worked on research projects this past year and the amount of time each person spent on research

2. The title of each research project and a brief description (a paragraph or two) of the research and its progress to date

3. Anticipated research projects for the coming year

4. Specific problems researchers faced this past year (insufficient budget, inadequate equipment, insufficient time, etc.)

Thank you.

cc: J. J. James

Memos are often hastily written without the writer's thinking through what is to be said. Because they are poorly planned, they are often much longer than necessary and don't communicate. Some rules of thumb for memo writing:

1. When in doubt, make it shorter rather than longer.

2. How you say what you say often causes more problems than what you say.

3. Follow the principles for readability outlined in chapter 7.

Writing a Newsletter

Two basic kinds of newsletters are those directed to employees and those directed outside the organization. Both must be well written and well designed. The difference between the two kinds is in the content, even though some organizations use one newsletter both for employees and for those outside the organization.

When writing newsletters, these questions must be answered:

What is the purpose of the newsletter? What do you want it to accomplish? Do you want it to inform employees of what's new in the organization, what new products are being produced, who has been promoted, who has been recognized for outstanding achievement? Do you want to inform customers of new products, special offers on products, special service information?

How often should the newsletter be written? This is an irrelevant question if your organization produces a monthly newsletter and you are expected to write it. But if you're just starting a newsletter, the question must be asked, and with it a series of related questions: Who will have responsibility for the newsletter? Will this person have enough time to produce a quality product along with his or her other responsibilities? If a newsletter is to be produced, it must be done well—particularly for external audiences because the newsletter often helps create an image for the organization.

What should be the content of the newsletter? If a newsletter is planned for the first time in an organization, the designated newsletter editor and management representatives should work out some broad guidelines about what content areas will be included. Will there be news about employee activities? Will there be regular features such as book reviews?

What will be the source of the content? One of the responsibilities of a newsletter writer is to solicit material for the newsletter. That means developing a system for obtaining material from those in the organization who have information to be shared in the newsletter. Sometimes considerable tact is necessary because people will expect their material to be printed exactly as they wrote it. To produce a quality newsletter, there must be consistency in style, and ordinary rules of readability must be followed. Much of the material turned in by contributors must be reorganized and rewritten simply because it doesn't fit the available space.

Will the newsletter include artwork? If so, you as a newsletter writer are probably responsible for writing the cutlines (captions for the artwork).

What system will you use to evaluate the effectiveness of the newsletter? Will you periodically ask those to whom the newsletter is sent to comment on the content and layout of the newsletter? If so, how? Include a survey form with the newsletter? Contact a select number of recipients and ask them questions about the newsletter? Or will you organize a newsletter editorial committee within the organization to review the newsletter and make suggestions for its improvement? Appendix 5 contains examples of two newsletters. The *Credit Union Leadership Letter,* an internal newsletter, is inexpensively printed and features information about people and places of interest to those connected with the organization. *Rituals of the Earth* is an external newsletter produced by the Sigurd Olson Environmental Institute. It contains information about institute activities of interest to those people it serves. Chapter 14 includes a reference with in-depth information about writing and producing newsletters.

Writing a Report

In the previous chapter laboratory reports and book reports were briefly discussed. Many professionals are called on to write longer, more comprehensive reports: progress reports, research reports, and analysis reports. As the name suggests, a progress report summarizes how a project or activity is proceeding. A research report may take a variety of forms, from the results of an experiment to the historical background of a particular event, product, or activity. An analysis report examines the various aspects of something, discussing each aspect in considerable depth. No matter what the type, reports have much in common with one another.

Organization

A formal report includes preliminary material, the body of the report, and sometimes an appendix.

The preliminary material comprises the following:

• A cover page, which shows the title of the report, the name of the person who prepared it, usually the name of the person or group to whom the report is submitted, and the date.

• A title page, which states the same information that was on the cover.

• A letter of transmittal, which shows the date, the name of the person to whom you are sending the report, reference to the title of the report, a brief comment about the scope of the report, a comment about those who may have assisted you with the report, and reference to any requests for the report.

• A table of contents, a topical outline of your report that helps your reader know where to look for specific information. The table of contents should correspond to the main heads and subheads you've used throughout the report.

• A table of illustrations, if applicable. List each illustration and its page number so your reader knows that you are using illustrations and where to find them quickly.

• An abstract, in which you briefly summarize the entire report in a few paragraphs. This may include the major findings, the conclusions you've reached, and the recommendations you're suggesting. Sometimes the abstract is placed immediately after the letter of transmittal so the reader can find it quickly.

The body of the report states what you have to say. Structure and organization, readability, and everything else discussed in previous chapters apply to the body of a report just as they apply to other nonfiction writing.

The appendix contains supporting information, such as letters received during the development of the report, survey forms, and graphic background, or supplementary material that doesn't relate directly to the text but helps the reader understand your report in total.

Mechanics

Many report writers overlook basic mechanics when they prepare reports.

1. Use 20-pound white bond paper, $8^1/2$ by 11 inches.

2. Double-space all typing except long quotations, which are indented and single spaced.

3. Use a $1^3/4$-inch left-side margin and a $1^1/2$-inch right-side margin so the report can be bound.

4. Leave $1^1/2$ inches at the top and 1 inch at the bottom.

5. Follow a consistent system for major heads and subheads. One system to follow is this:

First order: Center and underline.

<u>This Is a First-Order Head</u>

Second order: Center and do not underline.

This Is a Second-Order Head

Third order: Type flush left and underline.

<u>This Is a Third-Order Head</u>

Fourth order: Type flush left and do not underline.
This Is a Fourth-Order Head
Fifth Order: Underline and run into the paragraph, followed
by a period.
This Is a Fifth-Order Head. And now we begin . . .

6.   Make certain your typing is without error and the corrections
are not evident.

7.   Number all pages, including those in the introductory
material, in the center at the top or in the upper right-hand margin.
Never number in the upper left-hand margin because the binding
may cover the numbers. Two-sided typing is best with centered top
page numbers.

8.   Generally, type on one side of the page. In the interest of
paper conservation and thinner reports, you may occasionally type
on both sides. Make certain that the margins are maintained for
binding on all pages: wide margins on the left for right-hand pages,
wide margins on the right for left-hand pages.

9.   When using illustrations, make certain each one is given a
figure number and a caption. If used in the text, a figure must be
referred to, not simply included without explanation or reference.

Writing a Proposal

You write a proposal to persuade someone to do something—to
give you money for a new project, to accept a new idea you've
developed, to buy a new product or service, and so on. You will
generally write one of two kinds of proposal: (1) As a member of an
organization, you write a proposal to someone else in your organization. (2) As a member of an organization or as an individual, you
write a proposal to an outside agency or institution.

The basics for writing both kinds of proposal are essentially the
same. You work through a series of stages until the proposal is completed. The stages will vary depending on whether there is a prescribed format for the proposal. When the proposal format is prescribed, you are told what the major components of the proposal are,
the deadline dates, the forms to use for transmittal, the length of the
proposal, and what technical items should be considered (how the
budget should be presented, for instance). When the proposal format
is not prescribed, you can determine your own format, including the
components.

Stages in Proposal Development

1. Develop an idea. What do you want to propose? What is your idea? You need to answer a series of questions: How will your idea affect your organization? Will it result in new outlets for sales? Will it result in increased efficiency? Exactly who or what will benefit from your idea? Has your idea been tried before, either in your organization or in other organizations? If so, what were the results? Have other ideas been tried in the past to deal with the problem or the need toward which your idea is directed? If so, what were the results? What will be the short-term and the long-term benefits of your idea? What are the potential problems if your idea is implemented? How do the benefits of your idea outweigh the costs?

2. Select a funding source. (This step is irrelevant for a proposal developed for someone in your organization. If you are developing that kind of proposal, skip down to point 3.) The five common sources of funds for proposals are state agencies, federal agencies, private foundations (Ford, Kellogg, Rockefeller, Exxon, for example), business firms, and professional organizations.

To learn about possible sources of funding from a state agency, start by obtaining a copy of the state's agency listing. Select those agencies that appear to be closest to your proposal idea, and then write to them and ask about the availability of funds and whether they accept proposal applications. If there is any interest expressed, a personal visit to an agency is usually an important part of the procedure.

To search for possible funding sources in the federal government, consult the *Federal Register,* which is published five days a week and reports on government programs. The *Federal Register* usually includes a listing of topics on which a particular agency hopes to receive applications, a listing of eligible organizations and agencies, the criteria used in judging applications, the need for matching money (if any), and the deadline dates for proposal applications.

If you're interested in pursuing outside funding for your proposal from a foundation and wonder which foundation might be interested in your idea, check the following sources:

The *Foundation Directory* (The Foundation Center, Columbia University Press, 136 South Broadway, Irvington, NY 10533) is generally available on the reference shelves in large libraries. It is the basic reference guide to foundations, containing information on all the larger foundations. Foundations are listed by geographical areas as well as by fields of interest.

Foundation Grants Index (The Foundation Center, Columbia University Press, 136 South Broadway, Irvington, NY 10533) is a cumulative annual listing of foundation grants. Some material is also published periodically in the *Foundation News.*

Foundation News (Council on Foundations, P.O. Box 783, Old Chelsea Station, New York, NY 10011) is a bimonthly publication that lists foundation grants and information about foundation funding.

For those interested in proposals related to higher education, consult the *Chronicle of Higher Education,* a weekly publication that lists recent government and foundation grants to higher education institutions, as well as a summary of upcoming deadlines for government and foundation proposals.

In contacting business firms, it's wise to concentrate on those in your local community. They are usually most open to possible financing of proposals for their community.

To learn what's available from professional organizations, consult the *Encyclopedia of Associations* (Gale Research Company, Book Tower, Detroit, MI 48226). It includes the names, addresses, and purposes of associations; titles of major publications; and in some cases whether grant money is offered. Write a letter to a particular association to gain specific information.

3. Write a preproposal. A preproposal is merely a summary of your proposal idea. If you are writing a preproposal for someone within your organization with the intention of writing a more comprehensive proposal later on, a simple memo followed by a personal visit may be sufficient. If you are writing a preproposal for a possible funding source to see whether it might be interested enough in your idea to accept a comprehensive proposal, include the following information:

• A brief description of your idea

• Something about the uniqueness of your idea and its potential benefit to an organization, a community, or a specific group of people

• A request for additional information from the funding source about deadlines, guidelines for submitting proposals, ceilings on the amount of money offered, and of course whether the source would like to see a comprehensive proposal on the topic

Preproposals are time savers. Hours are spent writing proposals. By having an indication of interest for your idea as the result of a positive reaction to a preproposal, you can be assured that your comprehensive proposal will be studied thoroughly. The preproposal should be written as carefully as possible, for it must represent you and your idea. Also, some foundations and government agencies insist on preproposals and have guidelines that must be followed as well as deadlines for preproposal submissions.

Of course, if you have been asked to submit a proposal by your organization or by a foundation or government agency, you need not develop a preproposal but can immediately begin work on the comprehensive proposal.

4. Write the comprehensive proposal. If the foundation or agency has specific guidelines to be followed in preparing a proposal, follow them *to the letter.* If they do not have guidelines, the following is a list of the elements usually included in a proposal, whether it be directed within an organization or outside:

• A letter of transmittal. Include the name of the organization and person submitting the proposal, a concise summary of the need, the objectives, and the proposed program to meet the objectives. Also include a brief statement of the organization's interest in the project and its qualifications for carrying out the project. Indicate the names and addresses of persons who can be contacted for further information.

• A title page. Include the title of the project, the name of the applicant and the organization, and the date the proposal was prepared.

• A table of contents. Particularly for longer proposals, indicate the major sections of the proposal with page numbers.

• An abstract. In 250 words or less, summarize the project objectives, procedures, evaluation methods and indicators, and proposed application of the project's outcomes.

• A statement of the problem. Give a concise statement of what needs to be done and why. Reference is usually made to related projects or research on the topic and the successes and failures of these projects.

• Objectives. Tell what you plan the specific outcomes of the project to be. The objectives are usually listed and written in a way that they may be measured. For instance, one objective of a project about an exercise program for employees might be written: "To decrease employee sick days by 20 percent." The objectives must relate directly to the statement of the problem, indicating how each of the needs mentioned in the statement of the problem will be met.

• Procedures. Tell what will be done to meet the objectives. Sometimes this section begins with an overall statement about the approach for the project. This overall statement is followed by a specific listing of activities designed to meet each of the objectives. Procedures must include both what will be done and how it will be done. Sometimes it helps make the procedures clear if each objective is repeated in this section with an indication of the procedures that will be followed to meet the objective.

• Evaluation. Tell what procedures will be used to demonstrate the extent to which the objectives have been met. This section lists the type of evaluation information to be collected and how the information will be analyzed. The evaluation criteria for each objective are often also included in this section. For example, if an objective deals with changes in people, what minimum performance criteria will be acceptable? If your proposal outlines a procedure for training middle-management people in the use of microcomputers, what minimum performance will you accept as meeting the objective of your proposal?

• Dissemination. State what procedures you will follow to share what you learned with others. If your proposal is to try a new idea in a department within your organization, what approach will you use to let others know about the outcomes of your effort?

• Facilities and other resources. State whether any special facilities are required for your idea and how they will be provided. Sometimes special equipment is built into the budget for a proposal. In this section, the need for such special facilities can be explained.

• Personnel. Tell how many and what kinds of people will be necessary to carry out your proposal and how you will select them. Key people for the project should be tentatively selected at the time the proposal is submitted, and a brief description of their backgrounds and qualifications for working on the project should be included with the proposal.

• Budget. State the cost of the project and how much of the budget will go for which items: personnel, special equipment, travel, etc. If money is solicited from an outside source, tell how much of the budget is requested from the outside source and how much will be provided by your agency. Many funding agencies have specific requirements for the amount of money that must be matched by the organization submitting a proposal.

• Timetable. State what will happen and when. This is particularly important if your proposal is designed to take place over a period of more than one year. Many projects are designed to be conducted in phases, with a clear indication of the time period planned for each phase.

How Proposals Are Evaluated

Robert Lefferts[2] suggests eight criteria that funding agencies use most often to evaluate proposals:

• Clarity. The proposal should be organized so that the ideas presented follow one after the other. The style of writing should be simple and direct.

• Completeness. If the proposal is written to an agency that specifies guidelines, all the guidelines should be met. If no guidelines are offered, the standard elements of a proposal should be included.

• Responsiveness. The proposal should be consistent with what the agency or foundation says it is interested in funding.

• Internal and external consistency. All the elements of the proposal should be related and consistent with one another. The procedures should relate to the objectives, which in turn should relate to the identified need. The proposal should also be consistent with the findings of other projects of a similar nature, or it should make a case for a divergent approach.

• Understanding of the problem. The problem statement should clearly demonstrate an understanding of the problem the proposal addresses.

• Capability. The proposal should include evidence that the person or organization has the capability of carrying out the proposed program. This is demonstrated through the quality of the proposal itself, the backgrounds of the people involved, and the organization's history and reputation for doing similar kinds of activities.

• Efficiency and accountability. Funders want assurance that a program will be carefully managed and carried out. The timetable of activities is one way of demonstrating this to a funding source.

• Realism. A proposal must be realistic. It must be clear to the funding source that such a proposed program can be realistically carried out within the boundaries of the money and personnel requested.

NOTES

1. John Fielden, "What Do You Mean I Can't Write?" *Harvard Business Review,* May–June 1964, pp. 144–152.
2. Robert Lefferts, *Getting a Grant* (Englewood Cliffs, N.J.: Prentice-Hall, 1978).

Chapter 13

Writing for Publication

Why bother to write for publication, particularly if you have problems with your everyday writing requirements? People who write for publication give several reasons for doing so. Some say they write for publication because it allows them to reach a much larger audience than they could through face-to-face contact with individuals and groups. Some say they write for publication because it gives them personal satisfaction—they enjoy seeing their ideas in print. Still others say they write for publication because they enjoy the process of thinking through their ideas, putting them on paper, and then offering them to a wide audience for comment and criticism.

Many people who work in academia and certain other professions must write for publication because it's required of them if they want to advance in their professions or even keep their positions in some instances. (Moving from assistant to associate professor at a college or university usually requires a publication record.)

Finally, some writers offer practical reasons. Their published writing may help them achieve salary increases and promotions, for example. Or they write for publication because of the extra money they receive from their efforts. Work published in professional journals and scholarly publications rarely results in payment of any kind,

167

except perhaps in complimentary copies of the journal. But popular magazines do offer modest payment; and book publishing, particularly on popular topics, can result in sizable extra income.

In the following sections, writing and publishing nonfiction articles, book reviews, and books will be discussed.

Writing an Article for Publication

Three types of articles are common: popular, professional, and scholarly.

Popular Articles

Popular articles reach the largest number of people, often hundreds of times more people than can be reached by a scholarly journal (granted that the popular magazine and the scholarly journal have different purposes). Popular articles appear in the magazines you find on newsstands in supermarkets, airports, and drugstores across the country. They range from *Better Homes and Gardens, Woman's Day,* and *Reader's Digest* to the *Atlantic* and the *New Yorker.* Popular articles are written for a broad audience; they thus must be free of professional jargon and written as straightforwardly as possible. They must also be highly interesting because the competition for readership is great. People will read a paragraph or two of an article, and if it doesn't capture their interest, they'll move on to an article that does.

When writing a popular article, you should first consider what you are interested in. What do you know that others would like to know? Once you have selected a topic for your article, make sure it is sound. Will it appeal to a large number of people? Have other articles on this topic been published recently? You can find out by checking the *Readers' Guide to Periodical Literature* for the past five years to see whether similar articles have been published and, if so, where.

To find a magazine interested in publishing an article about your topic, check *Writer's Market,* the best single source of information on what sells to what kind of periodical and audience. The reference department in your local library should have a copy. Here are listed hundreds of magazines that purchase articles for publication, along with a description of the topics in which each magazine is interested, the length of articles wanted, and the payment levels. Also check *Writer's Digest* and the *Writer,* both monthly publications for free-lance writers that contain articles about writing as well as a list of publications that buy articles.

To find out the publication requirements of a particular magazine, study back issues of the magazine for at least six months. Note the range of articles published, the style of writing, the kinds of research done for the articles, the length of the articles, and whether the articles are written by magazine staff members or free-lancers. (You can figure that out by comparing the names of the editors listed in the front of the magazine with the authors of the articles listed in the table of contents.) You can also write directly to the magazine and request a copy of its suggestions for contributors. Most magazines have such guidelines available for potential contributors.

It is usually best not to submit an unsolicited completed manuscript to a popular magazine. First write a query to the magazine. A query is a letter written to an editor of a magazine that you believe should be interested in your article's topic. The query should include the following:

• The central idea of your article. Do not merely suggest a general topic; be as specific as possible. Don't suggest an article on microcomputers, but suggest how to use a microcomputer for word processing in the home or for home record keeping, or whatever your idea happens to be.

• The point of view you are taking. For example, if you're writing about management-employee relations in a small office, indicate whether you're writing from the employees' or the management's point of view. If you're writing about a controversial issue, indicate whether you will take a position on the issue or attempt to present both sides.

• The examples you use. Include one or two specific anecdotes that help make the point you'll present in your article.

• The research sources you use. Mention whether the article will be based on personal experience, interviews you've conducted, a mail survey, discussions with experts in the field, new research not yet in popular form, or whatever other sources you plan to use.

• Your qualifications for writing the article. If you have considerable experience in the area you're writing about, indicate it. If you have had other articles published, mention them.

The format for a query is a standard business-letter format. The items listed above need not be presented in any particular order, but all should be included in the letter. Make certain the query letter is written well, for an editor wants not only to learn about your idea for an article but also to see how well you write.

Rebecca E. Greer[1] offers the following tips for writing a query letter:

1.   Address your query letter to a specific editor. You can obtain the editor's name by consulting the magazine to which you plan to send the query.

2.   Keep the query letter to one page if possible, never more than two pages.

3.   Remember to write your query letter to the editor, not to the reader of your planned article. For instance, don't write in your query letter, "Here are six ways to accept a job layoff."

4.   Refer to yourself in the first person. Say, "I," not "the author" or "this writer."

5.   Mention the date when you believe you can deliver the manuscript. But be realistic and allow yourself sufficient time for conducting the necessary research and for writing and revising the article.

6.   If you've had something published in another magazine, include a copy of the published material. Do not include an article you wrote for your company newsletter or a letter you wrote to the editor of your local newspaper. Send only an article published in a magazine.

The advantages of submitting a query letter to an editor over submitting a completed manuscript are several. A query letter is a time-saver. It obviously doesn't take as long to prepare a query as it does to complete a manuscript. You also will hear from an editor more quickly with a query than with a manuscript. Further, the editor has an opportunity to make suggestions for your article if you present a query. The editor may suggest a different slant or a desired length for the article; he or she may even offer suggestions for content and research sources that you might not have been aware of. And if you receive a positive response to a query—a letter that says go ahead with the article—the chances of having your article accepted increase greatly over merely submitting the article without a query.

Generally, you will receive one of three responses to a query letter: (1) Sorry, we're not interested. (2) We might be interested if you will consider the following for your article. (3) Write the article and send it to us on speculation. (Speculation means the editor still has the right to turn down your article after it has been received.) If you receive either the second or the third response, research and write the article and send it to the editor whom you queried, indicating you are responding to an interest in the article.

Along with a positive response to your query letter, an editor often will send a copy of instructions to contributors that outline how the magazine wants article manuscripts submitted. Follow that style. If no such instructions are available, see Appendix 6, "Guidelines for Preparing Manuscripts."

Popular articles are usually reviewed by the editorial staff of the magazine. The staff considers the appropriateness of your topic for its publication, whether its magazine has recently published something on your topic or plans to in the near future, and the quality of your writing. Once again, you will receive one of three responses to your submission: (1) We like it and will publish it. (2) We won't publish it and are returning it. (3) We like it but want you to revise parts of it or add additional information. Unfortunately, you are most apt to receive the second response, a rejection. A rejection note is a carefully worded statement that politely says no. Language used in rejection slips includes the following:

"Thank you for letting us examine the enclosed material. I am returning it because our editorial board, after careful consideration, has decided that it does not meet our present editorial needs."

"We are sorry the enclosed material is not suited to our present needs."

"We regret that we are unable to use the enclosed material. Thank you for giving us the opportunity to consider it. The Editors."

One famous writer papered a wall with such rejection slips before publishing his first article. Think of them as status symbols.

Professional Articles

Professional articles are usually written *by* professionals *for* professionals, though sometimes free-lance writers write for both professional and popular magazines. Examples of professional magazines are *Lab World, Hospital Progress, Christian Ministry, Lifelong Learning,* and *Phi Delta Kappan.*

When writing an article for a professional magazine, you should first consider whether your idea will in some way assist the professionals for whom you are writing. Do you have an experience to share that other professionals could benefit from? Have you discovered a new approach to carrying out some aspect of your profession? Is your idea new?

To find professional magazines that might publish your article, first look to your own professional magazines, for those are the best prospects for your writing. Another source to check would be the *Directory of Publishing Opportunities,* 4th ed. (Chicago: Marquis Academic Media, 1979). This directory lists 3,400 specialist and professional magazines organized into 73 specific fields of interest. Besides names of editors and addresses, the directory includes editorial descriptions of the journals, manuscript requirements, circulation figures, and the time from acceptance of a manuscript to publication. Also check the *Standard Periodical Directory,* 7th ed., by Patricia Hagood (New York: Oxbridge Communications, Inc., 1980). Here is information on more than 65,000 United States and Canadian periodicals. The directory lists addresses, editors, publishers, and circulations and often mentions editorial content.

To find out about the editorial requirements of a particular professional magazine, write to the magazine and ask for a copy of its suggestions for contributors, just as you would do for a popular magazine.

In most instances, you should submit your completed manuscript to a professional magazine, not a query as suggested for popular magazines. However, you may want to write to a particular professional magazine beforehand to find out whether it accepts articles on a particular topic. Follow the guidelines for manuscript submission suggested in Appendix 6.

Often a professional magazine will have an editorial committee of professionals in the field who are asked to read manuscripts and make recommendations for publication. Occasionally a professional magazine will make in-house decisions (the editorial staff decides), but more often this procedure is not followed. Rather than sending a printed rejection slip that tells you little about how your article was received, a professional magazine editor will usually send you a letter with quotations from the reviewers telling you rather precisely why your article was rejected or what changes need to be made before it can be published.

Scholarly Articles

Scholarly articles are usually written *by* scholars *for* scholars to read. If the scholarly article is documenting scientific research, it will generally include the following components: (1) an abstract that includes a discussion of the research problem and a summary of related research on this topic; (2) an introduction, or a summary of how the research was conducted; (3) the findings; and (4) a discussion and implications section, which discusses what the findings mean and their implications for practice and for other research.

When writing a scholarly article, you should first consider whether your article will make a contribution to the literature of the discipline for which it is written. Is it original research that is based on a body of knowledge but either adds to or refutes the existing knowledge? Also, do you have the necessary background and training for writing a scholarly article? Most scholarly articles are written by researcher-scholars who have many years of formal training in the disciplines about which they are writing.

To find journals that might be interested in publishing a scholarly article, check the *Directory of Publishing Opportunities* and the *Standard Periodical Directory* discussed before. In addition, directories are available for certain disciplines. For instance, for psychology, psychiatry, and social work journals, you could consult the *Author's Guide to Journals in Psychology, Psychiatry, and Social Work,* edited by Allan Markle and Roger C. Rinn (New York: Haworth Press, 1977). Some 475 journals are listed here with information about editorial requirements, manuscript acceptance rates, topic orientations, and suggestions for manuscript submission.

For education journals, check the *Guide to Periodicals in Education and Its Academic Disciplines,* 2nd ed., by William L. Camp and Bryan L. Schwark (Metuchen, N.J.: Scarecrow Press, 1975). More than 600 journals are referenced here with information about accepted topics; suggestions for manuscript preparation, including style; as well as addresses, editors' names, and publication lag time.

For humanities journals, refer to the *Scholar's Market: An International Directory of Periodicals Publishing Literary Scholarship,* by Gary L. Harmon and Susanna M. Harmon (Columbus, Ohio: Ohio State University Libraries, 1974).

Of course, these are but a sampling of the directories available that list publication opportunities in the various disciplines.

To submit your manuscript, write to each journal and ask for its style sheet. Often the editors will indicate that they follow one of the standard styles for submitting articles, such as the *Publication Manual of the American Psychological Association,* the *Chicago Manual of Style,* published by the University of Chicago Press, or the *MLA Style Sheet,* published by the Modern Language Association of America. Some journals want you to submit two copies of the manuscript, others as many as three or four copies. Generally follow the same format for preparing scholarly articles as you would for preparing popular and professional articles (see Appendix 6).

Query letters are not used for scholarly articles. However, you may wish to write to a prospective journal to see whether it publishes articles in your research area.

Scholarly journals have editorial committees made up of scholars in the field who have responsibility for reviewing submitted manuscripts. Thus, scholarly journals are often referred to as juried or refereed journals. When the editor of a professional journal receives your manuscript, he or she quickly determines whether it generally fits the requirements of the journal. Then the manuscript is sent to three, sometimes as many as five, scholars who review it and make recommendations about its potential for publication. They make suggestions for revising the manuscript if they believe it has merit. If they judge it not acceptable, they offer reasons. An author almost never has a scholarly article accepted that does not require some revision. And because several people are involved in deciding about the manuscript, the time from submission to a decision is often considerable, sometimes several months.

The competition for publication in scholarly journals is as high as the standards; thus, the rejection rate for manuscripts submitted is great, often as high as 90 percent. For example, the rejection rate for the *Harvard Educational Review* is 95 percent; for the *Journal of Education,* 98 percent; and for the *American Education Research Journal,* 93 percent.[2]

Writing a Book Review for Publication

As noted before, a book review is much more than a book report. A book review not only summarizes what a book is about, but it also includes the subjective judgments of the reviewer concerning the quality of the book. Book reviews are a combination of objectivity and subjectivity. With too much of either one, the review can be seriously flawed.

The key to writing a good book review is knowing how to read a book critically. Reading a book critically takes time and usually means reading a book at least twice, and parts of it more than that. Unfortunately, some reviewers page through a book and pick up paragraphs here and there, which they then incorporate into their reviews. That is an affront to both the reader of the review and the author of the book. Both deserve a reviewer's careful attention to content.

How to Read Critically

Before you can make critical judgments about a book, you must understand what the author is saying. So the first time you read a book, read it for understanding, making notes in the margins and underlining sentences as you go along. To read for understanding, ask yourself the following questions:

What, in overview, is the book about? You should be able to state this in a sentence or two.

What question or questions is the author trying to answer in the book? One way to find out is to turn each chapter title and major heading into a question.

What answers does the author give to the questions?

What is the author's point of view? Sometimes the author will state explicitly the assumptions that have guided the work. Other times the reviewer has to ferret them out. Sometimes it's necessary to read other works by the same author to obtain a perspective on his or her point of view.

Once you understand the book, you are ready to read it critically. To read a book critically, search for both the shortcomings and the strengths of the work. Reflect on the questions the author was attempting to answer. Did the author answer all the questions? some of them? a few of them? Were some answered inaccurately in your opinion? If you feel the author's work was inadequate, what evidence do you have to back such a claim? Just as the author of a nonfiction work is obligated to support the positions taken in the work, so must a reviewer support positions taken in a review. As you read critically, you may wish to make notes with page references.

Once you've finished the second reading but before you begin writing the review, determine the length required by the selected magazine or journal. Some may accept only 250 words; others may want reviews of 1,000 or more words.

Some book reviewers work from a brief outline they've prepared of the main sections of the book, defining what the author was trying to accomplish and judging the success of the work. Others write the entire review without referring to an outline. They follow the developmental writing approach described in chapter 4, writing the entire review first and then carefully rewriting it to make sure both objectivity and subjectivity are maintained.

A common shortcoming of some reviewers is trying to impress the reader with their skill in discovering a flaw in a book and then skewering the author for the flaw. Mostly though, book reviews in professional magazines and scholarly journals are deadly boring.

The same principles for good writing must apply to book reviews as they do to all other forms of writing. Unfortunately, however, some book reviewers believe that no principles apply when writing a book review. Given this attitude, no wonder so many book reviews do not accomplish the important function they have. Many readers depend on reviews to describe and judge a new book so they can decide to check it out of the library, suggest it for a library purchase, buy it themselves, or order a copy for possible textbook use in a course or workshop. Book reviewers thus serve an extremely important function: introducing potential readers to books.

Writing a Book for Publication

You may consider writing one of three kinds of nonfiction books: a trade book, a professional book, or a textbook. First let's look at the characteristics of each.

Trade Books

Trade books are designed for the general public, though many are also used as textbooks and professional references. Many have become highly successful: Carl Sagan's *Cosmos,* Alvin Toffler's *Future Shock* and *The Third Wave,* Margaret Mead's works on anthropology, Will Durant's writings on philosophy, Isaac Asimov's nonfiction science books, Rollo May's and Carl Rogers's books on psychology, and Jerome Bruner's education books, for example.

Trade books must be written in a lively style that appeals to the general public as well as to other audiences, such as student groups. The author of a trade book runs the risk of being labeled a popularizer, a label that has been applied to many of the writers mentioned above. The label often comes from their professional peers who, in moments of jealousy, criticize a trade book as nonacademic. Yet the professional who is able to take complicated technical or research information and translate it for the general public should be applauded rather than criticized. The professionals who can share their knowledge with many groups of people help move a profession and a discipline forward by acquainting people outside it; they often provide the impetus for the interacting of disciplines rather than keeping information confined within a discipline.

Another characteristic of a trade book is the discount on trade books that publishers provide to bookstores. A trade book is usually discounted at 40 percent of the retail price of the book. For textbooks and professional books, the discount is often half that of the trade book amount, or 20 percent. That means bookstores display trade books more prominently and will likely keep them in stock longer. Some bookstores complain that the discount on textbooks and professional books is so low that they lose money in handling them. Many stores order textbooks based on a professor's anticipated class enrollments, and after the school year begins, the remaining textbooks are returned to the publishers.

Trade books may be hard cover, trade paperback, or mass-market paperback. The mass-market paperback books are usually those found on the racks in grocery stores, airports, drugstores, hotel lobbies, and the like.

Professional Books

Professional books are written for a more limited audience, a certain group of professionals such as lawyers, nurses, educators, business executives, or engineers. Whereas trade books are usually sold primarily through bookstores, professional books are marketed largely through the mail, journal advertising, and displays at conferences. Bookstores often carry professional books but in limited numbers, and they are often hidden away from the trade books because of the more favorable discount the store receives for trade books.

Textbooks

Textbooks are marketed almost entirely through college bookstores or by salespeople who visit schools and boards of education. While trade books and professional books are written for specific audiences, textbooks usually focus on a specific subject matter and present in-depth discussions of that subject, usually with discussion questions and sometimes with workbook exercises as well. Often a teacher's guide will accompany a textbook, with suggestions for using the textbook in the classroom. Textbooks are almost always written by authors who have considerable experience with the content area, often by teachers who have taught the subject.

Deciding on a Book Idea

Let's say you have an idea for a book and you want to find out whether you should move ahead with the idea and begin writing. Where do you start? The first thing to do is find out what other books exist on your topic and what slant these books have taken on it. (For most book topics, something already exists in print.) Go to your public library and check the current *Subject Guide to Books in Print.* In this reference volume, you'll find authors' names and titles of almost all the current books available in the United States. Once you've found titles of books related to your idea, find those books and see whether your idea is sufficiently different so that you should proceed.

If your idea is so different that you are convinced nothing like it has been published, this is the time to ask yourself whether anyone besides yourself would be interested in your book. In other words, who do you believe would buy your book? If you're able to answer positively the questions of differentness and marketability, you're ready to proceed with your book idea. The next step is to do some preliminary checking to see whether the information you need is available.

Before continuing, let's talk for a moment about dissertations. Many who finish graduate work look to the commercial publication of their dissertations and contact publishers with that goal in mind. That seems logical because the document has already been written and a graduate committee has approved it. It ought to be simple for a publisher to take the dissertation and publish it in book form. In a very few instances, that happens. But most of the time, it does not. By and large, publishers shy away from dissertations as they shy away from manuscripts by unknown poets.

As Peter Givler writes, "The dissertation is a kind of journeyman's badge. It announces to the academic world at large that you are capable of sustained research and scrupulous reasoning in your discipline. It signifies that you are now ready to profess your academic faith. . . .

". . . A dissertation, at the most reductive level, is written to pass muster with your committee and get you a degree. A scholarly book, on the other hand, locates you in the company of your peers; they expect you to speak to them with the voice, not of an apprentice, but an equal."[3]

So unless you are willing to completely rewrite your dissertation in book form, don't bother to contact a publisher about it—unless you truly have something that is different.

Finding a Publisher

I once had a student in a writing class who told me she was working on a book that was nearly completed and asked me which publishers should be allowed to publish her book. Unfortunately, the system doesn't work that way. True, there may be publishers interested in your book idea. But until you've become a published author (with a considerable reputation), you don't "allow" publishers to publish your work. You actively seek out one that can be persuaded to do so.

To find a publisher who might be interested in your book idea, consult the following:

Writer's Market (Cincinnati, Ohio: Writer's Digest Books) annually lists both book publishers and magazine publishers interested in buying free-lance submissions.

Book Publishers Directory (Detroit, Mich.: Gale Research Company) lists 4,500 publishing houses, including small presses, special-interest publishers, and association and government publishers in the United States and Canada.

Literary Market Place: The Directory of American Book Publishing (New York: R. R. Bowker) is one of the best annual references for finding the names and addresses of publishers, editors' names, information about books published, information about agents and writers' conferences, and more.

Publishers can be classified in various ways. Four kinds of publishers are national publishers, regional publishers, university presses, and professional organizations. National publishers market nationally; regional publishers tend to market within a region, such as New England or the upper Midwest; university presses, though usually national in focus, often emphasize more esoteric topics than the national and regional publishing houses; and professional organizations usually publish for their membership.

When deciding whether to submit your book idea to a particular publisher, consider whether the publishing house has published books similar to your own. Generally, a publishing house develops a line of books in a given area. For example, Jossey-Bass has a list of professional books in higher education, Follett has a list of books in adult and continuing education, and McGraw-Hill has a strong line of books for health professionals (each also publishes in other areas). Also consider whether the publishing house focuses on trade books, professional books, or textbooks. Some houses do all three. But many publishers who focus on textbooks have only a limited line of trade books, if any.

The Book Proposal

Once you've selected a potential publisher for your book idea, you're ready to make an initial contact. In most instances, do not send your completed manuscript as the initial contact with the publisher. It is far better to begin by sending a short letter asking whether the publisher might be interested in your book idea.

Preproposal Letter

The short letter, often called a preproposal letter, should contain the following:

- The theme or focus of your book idea.

- The potential market for your book, or who you believe will buy the book. Be as specific as you can, indicating numbers if possible. If you believe your book is particularly suited to nurses who head hospital continuing education programs, indicate the number of such nurses if you can.

- A mention of other books on your topic or a similar topic and how your book is different. Also mention how similar books have been accepted.

- Who you are and your qualifications for writing a book on this topic.

- Your publishing credits, if any.

- A remark that you will be happy to send a more complete proposal if the editor is interested in your book idea.

The purpose of the preproposal letter is to introduce yourself and your book idea to a book editor. The preproposal saves both you and the editor a lot of time. You'll usually hear from an editor promptly in reply to a preproposal letter. It often takes several weeks to receive a reply to a proposal letter and several months to receive a reply to a completed manuscript.

Detailed Proposal

Let's assume you've received a positive reply to your preproposal letter and a request from an editor for a detailed proposal. What do you include in the detailed proposal? (By the way, though it may in some instances be proper to send a preproposal letter to more than one publisher at the same time, it is not proper to send detailed proposals to more than one publisher at a time.)

A detailed proposal should contain the following:

- The basic idea for your book. Describe what your book will be about, its focus, and the kinds of research information you have available. Include a few examples of your research and personal experiences on your topic. Do all of this in a few paragraphs, not more than a double-spaced page of copy.

• The market for your book. Include a detailed account of the people who you believe will buy your book and why they will buy it. Include detailed numbers of the potential audience for the book. Indicate why you believe the book is of current interest. Does it discuss a topic that is on the minds of many people these days? Has this particular topic with this particular focus been unavailable to a group of people who have been asking for it? Do you have evidence of the need for this book, based on speaking engagements you've had, courses you've taught, or workshops you've led, and the accompanying requests from people for additional information?

• Similar books available. As best you can, list all the similar books available on your topic, indicating something of their content and how your book is different from them. Also, if you can obtain the information, mention how these books have been received by the audience you've identified above.

• Possible promotion for the book. If you believe your book will have appeal for book reviews, TV and radio interviews, or other promotions, mention them. If you give talks around the country on the topic of the book, indicate your willingness to promote your book as a part of your speaking engagements.

• Include a detailed chapter outline of your book and a list of chapter titles. Either list topics for each chapter or provide a paragraph or two of narration to indicate what each chapter is about.

• Research sources. Mention the research sources you have available. Include enough information about them to show the editor that you know how to do research.

• Your qualifications. Describe both your qualifications to write on the topic and your qualifications as a writer. Often it is wise to attach a brief vita of your employment and a list of published works.

• Sample chapters. Include two or three completed chapters of your book to indicate to the editor how you plan to handle the topic you've selected and to demonstrate your writing skills. Spend time on the sample chapters so they reflect your very best writing.

• Miscellany. Mention the anticipated length of your book (the approximate number of words) and indicate any illustrations you plan. Also indicate when you could have the manuscript completed.

Double-space the entire proposal, leave ample margins, put your name and address on the first page of the proposal, and number each of the pages. Be sure to keep a copy and send the proposal with a cover letter and a self-addressed, stamped envelope. Address the cover letter to the editor who responded to your preproposal letter and indicate that the detailed proposal is in response to an expressed interest in your book idea. You should hear in six weeks or so whether the publisher is interested in your book idea. If the publisher is not interested and you receive a rejection letter, send the proposal to the next publisher who expressed an interest in your preproposal. Sometimes you will contact several publishers before you find one interested in your idea. Don't give up until you've contacted at least a dozen publishers. Many best-sellers on the market today were turned down by several publishers before they were published.

The Book Contract

Let's assume the editor liked your detailed proposal and writes you the good news, saying a book contract will follow. What do you do when the contract arrives? Some authors are so elated at having their books accepted that they quickly mail back the contracts, scarcely reading the bold print to say nothing of the fine print. That can be a serious mistake, for even though the contract looks final, many of its clauses can be negotiated.

The least you should do is read your contract carefully, making certain you understand what each paragraph means. It's usually helpful to consult a friend who is a published book writer to discuss your contract. You may also want an attorney to review the contract with you.

The Authors Guild has a comprehensive pamphlet entitled *Your Book Contract,* which discusses in depth the various standard book contract clauses. The pamphlet is, however, available only to Authors Guild members. Once you've published your first book, contact the Authors Guild for membership information. (See chapter 14 for addresses and listings of source books on contract information.)

With even the most cursory glance at your book contract, you'll notice two items that involve money: the royalty payment schedule and an advance for your book. These often stand out because they are typed into the standard printed contract the publishing house uses. Sometimes before the contract is mailed to you, your editor will call you and ask whether a certain royalty schedule and a certain sum of money for an advance are satisfactory.

Although you may be led to believe that royalty schedules are standard in the book industry, that is far from the truth. Considerable variation exists, even within the same publishing house. There is also a difference in royalty schedules for trade books, professional books, and textbooks.

A typical royalty schedule for professional books and textbooks is 10 percent, sometimes 15 percent, on the net sum received from the sale of all copies. That means that you receive 10 percent of the amount the publisher receives for the book, not 10 percent of the retail price of the book. Let's say the book sells for $15, and the bookstore receives a 20 percent discount of $3. You thus receive 10 percent of $12, or $1.20 royalty for each book sold. Sometimes the royalty schedule is graduated, which means that after your book sells, say, 5,000 copies, you receive 15 percent royalty, or $1.80 per book sold.

Occasionally, a publisher of professional books and textbooks will follow a trade book royalty schedule based on the retail price of the book. That means, using the example above, that you receive $1.50 per book sold if the royalty schedule is 10 percent of the retail price. A typical trade book royalty is graduated as follows: 10 percent for the first 5,000 copies sold, 12½ percent for the next 5,000 copies sold, and 15 percent thereafter. Trade paperback books usually have a somewhat lower royalty schedule: 6 percent for the first 7,500 to 10,000 copies, with a possible increase to 7½ percent. Some offer a flat 7½ percent royalty; some start at 5 percent and increase slightly.

Usually royalties are reduced by 25 to 50 percent for export sales, say to Canada, for direct sales through the mail, and for copies of the book sold at discounts greater than 48 to 50 percent. The contract will spell out these details.

If you believe the royalty rates you are offered are not fair, raise a question about them with your editor. As a new author, however, you may need to be satisfied with the royalty rates offered you, particularly if they are comparable to what first-book authors are receiving. Royalties are usually paid twice a year, and the contract will indicate the payment dates.

The advance is a sum of money paid you prior to the publication of the book. It is usually paid in two installments, half when you sign the contract and half when you deliver your completed manuscript. Some publishers divide the payments into three parts: contract signing, manuscript delivery, and date of publication. The money you receive for an advance is subtracted from the royalties you will later earn. So, in effect, the advance is a loan against your royalties.

Advances will vary considerably. Some publishing houses, particularly smaller ones, offer no advances against royalties. On the other hand, you've probably heard of big-name authors receiving hundreds of thousands of dollars in advance money.

If this is your first book, you might realistically expect $500 to $2,000 in advance. The sum might be negotiated a bit higher if you can show your publisher you need the advance money to complete the research for your book.

Although space does not permit a detailed discussion of book contracts, following are several typical contract clauses and the importance of each.

• Manuscript form. A typical contract will ask for two copies of the manuscript, one original and one copy, typewritten, double spaced, with illustrations. Typically included in the manuscript form clause are these words: "Satisfactory in form and content to the publisher." If you received a contract based on a proposal and the final product doesn't come up to expectations, the publisher, under this clause, has the right to reject the manuscript. It is unusual for a publisher to invoke this clause, but it happens often enough that you need to be aware of it. If this happens to you, you may wish to negotiate whether you need to return the advance. The publisher may insist that you do. You may argue that you won't until you find another publisher for your manuscript.

• Date of delivery. Every book contract will have a scheduled date when the manuscript should be delivered. The publisher may reject your manuscript if you have broken the contract by delivering your manuscript late. Late delivery is a rather common problem among book authors, and it is often possible to receive an extension on your delivery date because of illness, difficulty in completing the research, etc. But if you simply deliver your manuscript a year late, you risk having it rejected. If your manuscript is more than two or three months late and you haven't negotiated an extension, you risk having your contract canceled and a demand that any advance money be returned.

• Author's warranty. You guarantee your publisher that your work is original—not plagiarized—and that none of the material is used without permission if the copyright is controlled by someone else. (The fair-use provision of copyright laws allows limited quoting without permission, as long as credit is given.) You also guarantee that your manuscript contains no libelous statements.

• Author's changes. Let's say that when you see your book in galley proofs, you decide you must add considerably more material to several of the chapters. Resist the urge to do so. This part of the contract usually includes a statement such as, "Any changes the author makes that cost more than 10 percent of the total cost of composition will be charged against the author's royalty account."

• Competing work. This clause forbids you to write a book for another editor or publisher that would compete directly with the book under contract.

• Options. This clause grants to your publisher the first look at a succeeding book you may do. For nonfiction books, it makes sense to delete this clause. If you've had a bad experience with a publisher, or if you feel your book hasn't been marketed or edited well, you can quickly move to another publisher if this clause is absent.

Submitting the Book Manuscript

Generally, the same procedure for submitting a manuscript to a magazine or journal applies to a book. Most book publishers have either books or pamphlets that outline their style requirements, or they refer you to a standard reference such as the *Chicago Manual of Style,* published by the University of Chicago Press.

Generally, at the same time you submit the manuscript, you should include the original permissions letters you've obtained for copyrighted material in your manuscript. Keep copies for yourself. It is your responsibility as the author to obtain the necessary permissions (see Appendix 2 for a sample permissions request).

Reading Proof

In contrast to magazine publishing, you will be asked to proofread the galley proofs or the page proofs of your book. Although this is a tedious and time-consuming process, it is essential you take the project seriously. You are searching for composition errors that may have been missed by the professional proofreaders who also correct the work.

The most accurate way to proofread is for the author of the work and another person to work together, one reading aloud from the edited manuscript and the other following along with the galley or page proofs. Sometimes when you read the printed pages silently, obvious errors are overlooked. When an error is discovered, mark the correction using standard proofreader's marks (see Appendix 6).

Preparing an Anthology

Two kinds of anthology are commonly prepared: those that are a collection of previously published materials and those that are a collection of original materials. The author of an anthology becomes an editor who selects either the material to be included if published materials are involved or contributors if original contributions are sought. Although it sounds like an easy way to write a book, it usually turns into a difficult, extremely time-consuming project. (For an anthology of previously published works, the most time-consuming part of the project is obtaining the necessary permissions from the publishers involved.) Also, many publishers are not interested in publishing anthologies, so it is particularly important for the author-editor to develop a proposal and obtain interest in an anthology before proceeding with it.

In addition to obtaining permissions and either physically organizing a manuscript that consists in large measure of photocopies of published works or editing and retyping original contributions, you are obligated to develop a focus for the anthology. Sometimes that involves writing introductions to the parts of the book; sometimes it means writing a book introduction that outlines what you are attempting to accomplish with the anthology. Your role as an editor is thus much more than collecting published or original material from a variety of sources and assembling them in a manuscript.

Your success in developing a focus for the anthology that ties the entire project together is the key to whether the anthology will be more than just another collection of disparate articles with your name affixed as editor.

Collaboration

Sometimes it makes sense to write a book with a colleague. It makes a project less formidable if the writing tasks can be divided. Collaboration also provides an additional perspective and a breadth of knowledge and insight greater than when one person does all the work. For some people, the task of book writing is extremely lonely. Collaboration allows for personal interaction as a part of the writing process.

Collaboration, however, is not without its disadvantages. One of the most obvious disadvantages is the possibility that you may not get along with your colleague. Nothing sours a writing project more quickly than a personality conflict between joint authors. Collaboration requires many hours for discussion of the project and decisions about who's going to work on what, what content should be in the book, and so on. If collaborators happen to live in opposite parts of the country, geographical distance can be a serious problem, particularly if extended discussions are necessary during the writing process. Still another disadvantage is the differing writing speeds of the collaborators. If you can produce a chapter in rough draft in a week and your colleague requires a month, your project will likely face problems.

A practical way to solve some of these problems is to decide on a senior collaborator, the person whose name will appear first on the book cover. The senior collaborator should be responsible for making the hundreds of little decisions about the development of the book without always feeling a need to consult the other collaborator(s). And if there is a disagreement among collaborators, the senior collaborator should be responsible for resolving the disagreement.

Agents

You've probably heard that if you want to find a publisher for your book, you first must find an agent. A literary agent is someone who specializes in placing authors' manuscripts with book publishers and, in some cases, with magazine publishers as well. For this service, the literary agent receives a commission of 10 percent (sometimes 15 percent) of everything an author receives from a publisher—10 percent of both the advance and the royalties.

If you're writing fiction, it is almost essential that you find an agent to offer your work. But if you're writing nonfiction, which is the emphasis of this book, you can do quite well without an agent. In fact, as a beginning book writer, you'll have some difficulty finding an agent. Agents generally want to work with established authors. (To find a list of the names and addresses of literary agents, consult the *Literary Market Place,* cited in chapter 14.)

Some so-called agents advertise widely in writing magazines and charge fees for reading and offering advice on how to revise your work. As you might guess, these persons make their money from your fees and are not dependent on selling your manuscript to a publisher. Avoid them. If you want help with your completed manuscript, consult the resource section in chapter 14. You can generally find someone to assist you with the revision of your manuscript at a fee considerably less than that charged by the agents who advertise in writing magazines.

If you follow the procedures for developing a book proposal suggested in this chapter and you have a book idea that has market potential, you will have a good chance of marketing your book. In some instances, you have a better chance than that offered by a literary agent, for you may know which publishers publish books in your area of interest better than a literary agent does.

Subsidy and Self-Publishing

Let's say you've developed your proposal, sent it to a dozen or more publishers, and have been turned down by all of them. Let's also assume that you still believe strongly in your book and know it will sell if only given a chance. What options do you have? At least two. You can have a subsidy publisher publish your book for you, or you can publish it yourself.

Subsidy Publishing

Subsidy publishing means you pay to have your book published rather than being paid by the publisher. If you study the writing magazines, you'll notice ads from subsidy publishing houses such as Vantage Press, Dorrance and Company, and Exposition Press. These publishers will work with your manuscript, edit it, provide artwork at times, do the printing and binding, and provide completed, attractive books.

Unfortunately, the author usually does not sell enough copies of his or her subsidy-published book to recoup the investment made in publishing it.

Self-Publishing

In most instances, when you cannot find a commercial publisher for your book and yet you believe in what you have written, it is less expensive to publish the book yourself. Thousands of people are doing this. Any middle-size or larger city has printers who are happy to do the printing and binding for your book. Most cities have freelance editors who will do the editing for hire. Unfortunately, the problem is usually marketing. How do you go about marketing your self-published book? Three obvious things you can do: visit the bookstores in your area and ask them to stock your book, run ads in professional magazines read by people you believe would be interested in your book, and develop a mailing list of people who you believe would be interested in your book, perhaps the membership list of the professional organization to which you belong. Check chapter 14 for books about how to self-publish.

One of the major differences between subsidy publishing and self-publishing is control. In self-publishing, the author finances, owns, and distributes his or her books. In subsidy publishing, the author finances, but the publisher owns and distributes the books.

NOTES

1. Rebecca E. Greer, "How to Query an Editor," *Writer's Digest,* 1973.
2. Raymond J. Rodriques and Donald M. Uhlenberg, "Publish? or Perish the Thought?" *Journal of Teacher Education,* July–August 1978, p. 65.
3. Peter Givler, "Notes from an Acquiring Editor," *Imprimenda: A Publication of the University of Wisconsin Press,* October 1980.

Chapter 14

Resources

Writing Log

An important resource introduced earlier in the book is your Writing Log. In addition to the activities suggested earlier, consider doing the following:

1. Write the reactions you have gotten from others and your own reactions to a writing project you've recently completed. Compare the reactions you received from others on this project with the reactions you received about a similar project that was written before you began working on improving your writing skills.

2. Continue listing words that you have difficulty spelling.

3. Write an assessment of your progress toward completing your learning plan, indicating the extent to which you solved the learning problems you identified in your initial writing skills inventory.

4. Write a new learning plan, identifying problem areas you still have. Put this in your Writing Log for future reference.

Developing a Learning Plan

For more information about how to plan and carry out your own learning project, consult the following:

Gross, Ronald. *The Lifelong Learner.* New York: Simon and Schuster, 1977. Gross offers several case studies of people who have planned their own learning projects. He includes criteria for selecting an approach to learning and guidelines for planning and carrying out a personal learning project.

Knowles, Malcolm S. *Self-directed Learning: A Guide for Learners and Teachers.* New York: Association Press, 1975. Here are suggestions for designing a learning plan, including how to select resources such as workshops, seminars, readings, and one-to-one consultation.

Smith, Robert. *Learning How to Learn: Applied Theory for Adults.* Chicago: Follett, 1982. A guidebook for planning and carrying out personal learning projects.

Tough, Allen. *The Adult's Learning Projects.* Toronto: The Ontario Institute for Studies in Education, 1971. Tough has researched self-directed learning for many years. This book includes such topics as how learners do self-planning and the kinds of learning projects people carry out by themselves.

Writing Skills Books

The following books provide basic information on improving writing skills:

Bates, Jefferson. *Writing with Precision.* Washington, D.C.: Acropolis Books, 1978. Covers self-editing, writing concisely, using action verbs, and organizing to write.

Berry, Thomas Elliott. *The Craft of Writing.* New York: McGraw-Hill, 1974. Focuses on the writing process, planning, paragraph writing, and how to write description, narration, exposition, and argument.

Flesch, Rudolf. *The Art of Readable Writing.* New York: Harper & Row, 1949. An excellent book. Flesch covers such topics as shaping ideas, developing an ear for writing, and learning how to operate a blue pencil. He believes that all writing is creative and that we should develop a knack for including drama in everyday prose.

Flesch, Rudolf, and Lass, A. H. *A New Guide to Better Writing.* New York: Harper & Row, 1949. Topics covered include starting to write, putting your ideas in order, tying ideas together, talking to your reader, saving your reader extra work, and making writing fun to read. Also included are basic tips on writing sentences, giving writing punch, selecting correct adjectives and adverbs, and finding the right word.

Hersey, John, ed. *The Writer's Craft.* New York: Alfred Knopf, 1974. A collection of articles on a variety of topics of interest to the writer. Hersey says writing is a craft and requires skills that can be learned. He emphasizes that writers must love words.

Miller, Casey, and Swift, Kate. *The Handbook of Nonsexist Writing.* New York: Lippincott & Crowell, 1980. Tips for finding alternatives to the generic *man,* approaches to solving the third-person pronoun problem, and other practical suggestions for taking sexism out of writing.

Rivers, William. *Writing: Craft and Art.* Englewood Cliffs, N.J.: Prentice-Hall, 1975. Rivers emphasizes how to outline and organize writing, approach revision, select the right word, and more.

Shaw, Fran Weber. *Thirty Ways to Help You Write.* New York: Bantam Books, 1980. Through a series of exercises, Shaw discusses how to describe people, places, and things; how to find your way from notes to a first draft; and how to become your own best editor.

Shew, Phillip, and Pincar, Debra. *Writing Skills.* 2nd ed. New York: McGraw-Hill, 1980. A programmed learning format designed for the reader to carry out various exercises on such topics as writing sentences, building paragraphs, organizing essays, and rewriting and editing.

Zinsser, William. *On Writing Well.* New York: Harper & Row, 1980. An enjoyable, easy-to-read book that includes such topics as simplicity, clutter, style, interviewing, writing about a place, science writing, technical writing, and writing for your job.

Writing Courses

For information about writing courses and workshops, consult the following:

Cross, Wilbur. *The Weekend Education Source Book.* New York: Harper's Magazine Press, 1976. A guide for finding writing courses in your community, with information about how to contact adult education providers such as colleges, universities, and others.

Cushing, David. "Reading, Writing, and Listening Courses," *Training,* vol. 18, no. 2, February 1981, pp. 52–54. How to choose the right reading, writing, and listening course.

Draves, Bill. *The Free University.* Chicago: Follett, 1980. Draves includes a national directory of free universities and learning networks, many of which offer courses and workshops in writing skills improvement. (A free university is one that offers noncredit classes to the general public.)

Elbow, Peter. *Writing Without Teachers.* New York: Oxford University Press, 1973. How to set up a writing class without a teacher, with participants sharing and critiquing each other's writing.

For information about credit, noncredit, and independent study courses, contact the colleges and universities in your community.

Writers' Conferences

Following are examples of writers' conferences held each year. Write to the conference director at the address given for more details.

Professional Writing Workshop, English Dept., P.O. Box 248145, University of Miami, Coral Gables, FL 33124.

Mississippi Valley Writers Conference, College Center, Augustana College, Rock Island, IL 61201.

Midwest Writers Workshop, Ball State University, Muncie, IN 47306.

Eastern Writers Conference, English Dept., Salem State College, Salem, MA 01970.

Upper Midwest Writers Conference, Box 48, Bemidji State University, Bemidji, MN 56601.

ASJA Writers Conference, American Society of Authors and Journalists, 5101 Broadway, Suite 1907, New York, NY 10036.

Chautauqua Writers Workshop, Box 28, Chautauqua Summer School, Chautauqua, NY 14722.

Cuyahoga Writers Conference, Cuyahoga Community College Eastern Campus, 25444 Harvard Rd., Cleveland, OH 44122.

Short Course on Professional Writing, Comprehensive Program, University of Oklahoma, Room 126, 1700 Asp, Norman, OK 73037.

Southwest Writers Conference, University of Houston, Continuing Education, 4800 Calhoun, Houston, TX 77004.

Bread Loaf Writers Conference, Middlebury College, Middlebury, VT 05753.

Rhinelander School of Arts, Extension Arts Development, 610 Langdon St., Madison, WI 53706.

For additional information about writers' conferences, consult the May issues of the *Writer* (8 Arlington St., Boston, MA) and *Writer's Digest* (9933 Alliance Rd., Cincinnati, OH). Also, *Literary Market*

Place (New York: R. R. Bowker, published annually) includes a list of writing conferences that are conducted annually.

National Writers' Groups

Following are examples of national writers' groups. Write to them for membership information. Also consult the *Writer's Market* (Cincinnati, Ohio: Writer's Digest Books) for a more comprehensive list of writers' organizations.

American Society of Journalists and Authors, 1501 Broadway, Room 1907, New York, NY 10036.

Associated Business Writers of America, 1450 S. Havana St., Aurora, CO 80012. For those writers interested in advertising copy, public relations, reports, or business and technical writing. Includes members, who are full-time writers, and associates, who write but also have other responsibilities.

The Authors Guild, 234 W. 44th St., New York, NY 10036. For writers who have been published.

National League of American Pen Women, Inc., 1300 17th St., N.W., Washington, D.C. 20036. Holds state and national meetings.

National Writers Club, Inc. 1450 S. Havana, Aurora, CO 80012. Associate membership open to anyone seriously interested in writing.

Research Approaches

For those interested in commonly followed research approaches in the social sciences, including conducting surveys and case studies, interviewing, selecting random samples, and using statistics, consult the following:

Fox, David J. *The Research Process in Education.* New York: Holt, 1969.

Kerlinger, Fred N. *Foundations of Behavioral Research.* New York: Holt, 1964.

Schatzman, Leonard, and Strauss, Anselm L. *Field Research.* Englewood Cliffs, N.J.: Prentice-Hall, 1973.

Simon, Julian. *Basic Methods in Social Science.* New York: Random House, 1969.

Other useful resources for researching include the following:

Barzun, Jacques, and Graff, Henry F. *The Modern Researcher.* 3rd ed. New York: Harcourt Brace Jovanovich, 1977. An excellent book for those writers interested in historical research and how to do it. Included are chapters on finding facts, verification, handling ideas, and truth and causation. Approximately half the book is devoted to writing, including organizing, writing clear sentences, and quoting and translating.

Brady, John. *The Craft of Interviewing.* Cincinnati, Ohio: Writer's Digest Books, 1976. An easy-to-read guide to interviewing with lots of personal anecdotes.

McCormick, Mona. *Who-What-When-Where-How-Why-Made Easy.* New York: Quadrangle Books, 1971. All about finding and using reference books, including how to use a library reference area.

Rivers, William L. *Finding Facts.* Englewood Cliffs, N.J.: Prentice-Hall, 1975. A how-to guide for finding and interpreting information. Rivers includes chapters on interviewing and observing and contrasts research approaches used by historians, literary researchers, and social scientists.

Sheehy, Eugene P. *Guide to Reference Books.* Chicago: American Library Association, revised periodically. An indispensable guide to references that lists 10,000-plus titles.

Grammar and Style

Barzun, Jacques. *Simple and Direct.* New York: Harper & Row, 1976. Barzun emphasizes which words to use, how to link them, what meaning to communicate, and what impression a piece of writing will make.

Bernstein, Theodore M. *Miss Thistlebottom's Hobgoblins.* New York: Farrar, Straus and Giroux, 1971. A cleverly written guide to avoiding common writing errors. Some of the topics include a word to the whys, witchcraft in words, syntax scarecrows, imps of idioms, and spooks of style.

————. *Watch Your Language.* New York: Atheneum, 1965. How to keep an eye out for misplaced words and wordiness. Chapter 4, "Helpful Hints for Hatchet Men," is a guide to revising and rewriting.

Ehrlich, Eugene, and Murphy, Daniel. *Basic Grammar for Writing.* New York: McGraw-Hill, 1967. The book begins with a self-testing exercise on grammar and goes on to cover such basics as sentence structure, use of verbs, and punctuation.

Gould, Alan J. *Writing for the AP.* New York: Associated Press, 1959. Using many examples, Gould talks about readability, words, leads, sentences, technique, and color in writing.

Gowen, James A. *English Review Manual: A Program for Self-Instruction.* New York: McGraw-Hill, 1980. Using a programmed learning format, Gowen covers sentences, verbs, nouns, pronouns, modifiers, illogical and incomplete constructions, and punctuation.

Graves, Robert, and Hodge, Alan. *The Reader over Your Shoulder: A Handbook for Writers of English Prose.* New York: Random House, 1971. The book includes twenty-five principles for good writing, including the following: "No unnecessary idea, phrase or word should be included in a sentence." "There should never be any doubt left as to how many." "There should never be any doubt left as to when."

Hodges, John C., and Whitten, Mary E. *Harbrace College Handbook.* 8th ed. New York: Harcourt Brace Jovanovich, 1977. An excellent reference book for the writer's desk. Here are included such topics as when to use commas and how to handle pronouns, as well as sentence structure and editing for wordiness.

Langan, John. *Sentence Skills.* New York: McGraw-Hill, 1979. In a programmed format, this book covers such topics as correct grammar, punctuation, word use, and mechanics of writing.

The Chicago Manual of Style. 13th ed. Chicago: University of Chicago Press, 1982. The classic style manual used by many writers and editors. An excellent reference.

The MLA Style Sheet. 2nd ed. New York: Modern Language Association of America, 1970. A brief but useful style book.

Morsberger, Robert E. *Commonsense Grammar and Style.* 2nd ed. New York: Thomas Y. Crowell, 1972. Includes a number of exercises for the reader on basic grammar and a brief history of English grammar.

Newman, Edwin. *Strictly Speaking.* New York: Bobbs, Merrill, 1974. Newman is concerned about the degeneration of the English language and offers suggestions about what writers need to do. The writing is interesting and entertaining.

Ross, Stephen V. *Spelling Made Simple.* Garden City, N.Y.: Doubleday, 1981. An emphasis on analyzing spelling weaknesses and mastering the most frequently misspelled words. The book is designed for self-study with many exercises.

Safire, William. *On Language.* New York: Times Books, 1980. Word usage, style, jargon, and even something on word origins.

Shaw, Harry. *Errors in English: And Ways to Correct Them.* 2nd ed. New York: Barnes and Noble, 1970. Organized in a dictionary format. Shaw includes guides to correct usage, correct sentence structure, spelling, punctuation, grammar, and composition.

Strunk, William Jr., and White, E. B. *The Elements of Style.* 2nd ed. New York: Macmillan, 1972. No writer should be without this classic. Everything from rules of usage and elementary principles of composition to words and expressions commonly misused.

Waldhorn, Arthur, and Zeigler, Arthur. *English Made Simple.* Rev. ed. Garden City, N.Y.: Doubleday, 1981. A series of exercises on such topics as sentences, paragraphs, punctuation, vocabulary building, and style.

Writing for Educational Assignments

Apps, Jerold W. *Study Skills: For Those Adults Returning to School.* Rev. ed. New York: McGraw-Hill, 1982. Includes ideas for writing all the commonly required writing that students encounter, from term papers to dissertations. Exercises and self-study suggestions are included.

Deese, James, and Deese, Ellin K. *How to Study.* 3rd ed. New York: McGraw-Hill, 1979. Includes chapters on taking examinations and writing papers.

Glorfeld, Louis E.; Lauerman, David A.; and Stageberg, Norman C. *A Concise Guide for Writers.* 2nd ed. New York: Holt, Rinehart and Winston, 1969. Suggestions for writing themes and basic student compositions.

Langan, John, and Nadell, Judith. *Doing Well in College.* New York: McGraw-Hill, 1980. How to write essay exams, book reports, and research reports.

Mulkerne, Donald J. D., and Kahn, Gilbert. *The Term Paper: Step by Step.* Rev. ed. New York: Anchor Books, 1977. From choosing and limiting the subject, making an outline, and writing the paper to footnoting and final typing.

Pauk, Walter. *How to Study in College.* Boston: Houghton Mifflin, 1974. Chapters on writing exams, term papers, and research reports.

Riebel, John P. *How to Write Reports, Papers, Theses, Articles.* 2nd ed. New York: Arco, 1972. Begins with approaches to thinking and collecting factual information and proceeds to suggestions for writing and drawing conclusions.

Turabian, Kate. *A Manual for Writers of Term Papers, Theses, and Dissertations.* 4th ed. Chicago: University of Chicago Press, 1973.

_____. *Student's Guide for Writing College Papers.* Chicago:
University of Chicago Press, 1976. Both Turabian books are
excellent guides for students on writing footnotes, bibliographies,
headlines—all the mechanics of good writing. They also offer
much practical information about choosing a topic, collecting
material, and planning and writing papers.

Writing for Professional Requirements

Bates, Jefferson D. *Writing with Precision.* Washington, D.C.:
Acropolis Books, 1978. How to write letters, memos, and
regulations clearly and precisely. How to write like a professional.

Blumenthal, Lassor A. *Successful Business Writing.* New York:
Grosset and Dunlap, 1976. Writing sales letters, collection letters,
letters of inquiry, complaint letters, memos, proposals,
presentations, and resumes.

Hall, Mary. *Developing Skills in Proposal Writing.* Corvallis, Oreg.:
Office of Federal Relations, Oregon State System of Higher
Education, 1971. From idea to review, Hall discusses the
development of proposals. An excellent guide on writing
proposals for outside funding agencies.

Lefferts, Robert. *Getting a Grant.* Englewood Cliffs, N.J.: Prentice-
Hall, 1978. Suggestions for proposal writing. Also describes how
grant proposals are evaluated.

Schuh, Colleen. *Newsletters: Designing and Producing Them.*
Madison, Wis.: Division of Program and Staff Development,
University of Wisconsin–Extension, 1978. Ideas about writing
and designing attractive newsletters by an instructor of the topic.

Writing for Publication

Almost every library has a collection of how-to books for writers or
would-be writers interested in publication. Below is a sample of these
materials. Check with your library for additional books.

Applebaum, Judith, and Evans, Nancy. *How to Get Happily
Published.* New York: Harper & Row, 1978. The emphasis here is
on finding a publisher, using an agent, submitting completed
manuscripts, and self-publishing. The material is most useful to
those interested in book writing.

Apps, Jerold W. *Tips for Article Writers.* Madison, Wis.: Wisconsin
Regional Writers, 1973. Basic suggestions for developing and

writing articles for publication. Some information on marketing approaches.

Authors Guild, 234 W. 44th St., New York, NY. A professional organization of published book writers that offers information on contracts, copyrights, and many other topics. You must be a member of the guild to receive its materials.

Balkin, Richard. *A Writer's Guide to Book Publishing.* New York: Hawthorn Books, 1977. Topics include how to approach a publisher, how a publisher evaluates a proposal or a manuscript, how to understand and negotiate a book contract, how a manuscript is turned into a finished book, and how a publisher markets a book. A good, practical guide for those interested in book publishing.

Davidson, Marion, and Blue, Martha. *Making It Legal.* New York: McGraw-Hill, 1979. How to prevent legal problems. Includes tax information for writers and basic information about book contracts.

Drewry, John E. *Writing Book Reviews.* Rev. ed. Boston: The Writer, 1966. Suggestions for writing a competent book review.

Goodman, Joseph V. *How to Publish and Sell Your Book: A Guide for the Self-Publishing Author.* 4th ed. Chicago: Adams Press, 1977. Practical suggestions and pitfalls to avoid when publishing your own book.

Gunther, Max. *Writing and Selling a Non-Fiction Book.* Boston: The Writer, 1973. Basic suggestions for the beginning book writer.

Hanson, Nancy Edmonds. *How You Can Make $20,000 a Year Writing.* Cincinnati: Writer's Digest Books, 1980. Basic suggestions for both magazine and book writing.

Jacobs, Hayes B. *Writing and Selling Non-Fiction.* Cincinnati: Writer's Digest Books, 1967. An excellent basic book for those interested in publishing their writing. Includes information about book as well as magazine writing.

Karp, Irwin. *What Authors Should Know.* New York: Harper & Row, 1978. The counsel to the Authors' League of America offers advice on copyright law, contracts, libel, and invasion of privacy.

Meredith, Scott. *Writing to Sell.* New York: Harper & Row, 1974. Emphasis is on selling what you have written. Meredith is a New York agent and offers much practical advice on how to approach possible markets.

Neal, Harry Edward. *Nonfiction: From Idea to Published Book.* New York: Funk and Wagnalls, 1964. Neal says that to be a successful writer you must be "literate, curious, enthusiastic, and persevering." He offers basic suggestions for nonfiction book writing.

Polking, Kirk, and Meranus, Leonard S. *Law and the Writer.* Cincinnati: Writer's Digest Books, 1981. Emphasis on recognizing and avoiding legal problems before they occur. Includes complete text of copyright law.

Publishers Weekly, 1180 Avenue of the Americas, New York, NY 10036. The most up-to-date information available about publishing facts, figures, ideas, and people. A weekly listing of new books, both fiction and nonfiction.

Readers' Guide to Periodical Literature. New York: H. W. Wilson Company, published annually. Standard reference to determine what has been published in a periodical on a topic. A starting place for many writers who need to know who has already written on the topics in which they are interested.

Schoenfeld, Clarence A. *Effective Feature Writing.* New York: Harper & Row, 1960. The what, why, and how of article writing, plus information about marketing. An excellent source book.

Subject Guide to Books in Print and *Subject Guide to Forthcoming Books.* New York: R. R. Bowker, published periodically. Reference books that help writers of books know what has been published or will soon be published on topics in which they are interested.

Van Til, William. *Writing for Professional Publication.* Rockleigh, N.J.: Allyn and Bacon, 1980. How to write for professional journals and scholarly journals and how to write book reviews, textbooks, trade books, and professional books. Includes a list of authors' guides to scholarly periodicals.

The Writer. 8 Arlington Street, Boston, MA. A monthly magazine with much practical advice for writers on writing as well as on marketing.

Writer's Digest. 9933 Alliance Road, Cincinnati, OH. Provides information on both marketing and improving writing. Published monthly.

Writer's Market. Cincinnati: Writer's Digest Books, published annually. A comprehensive listing of publishers, both magazine and book, that purchase free-lance material. Cites editorial requirements and rates of payment. Thousands of publishing opportunities listed.

Forms for Developing a Learning Plan

Writing Skills Inventory*

	Weak	Fair	Strong	Don't Know	Not Relevant
Research skills					
Using libraries	⎯	⎯	⎯	⎯	⎯
Interviewing	⎯	⎯	⎯	⎯	⎯
Using surveys	⎯	⎯	⎯	⎯	⎯
Observing	⎯	⎯	⎯	⎯	⎯
Skills in writing—					
Beginnings	⎯	⎯	⎯	⎯	⎯
Endings	⎯	⎯	⎯	⎯	⎯
Organization skills	⎯	⎯	⎯	⎯	⎯
Skills for writing—					
Description	⎯	⎯	⎯	⎯	⎯
Narration	⎯	⎯	⎯	⎯	⎯
Explanation	⎯	⎯	⎯	⎯	⎯
Criticism	⎯	⎯	⎯	⎯	⎯

* If some of the skills listed are unfamiliar, explanations can be found elsewhere in the book by checking the Index.

	Weak	Fair	Strong	Don't Know	Not Relevant
Persuasion	——	——	——	——	——

Skills for readable writing, using—

The active voice	——	——	——	——	——
Precise words	——	——	——	——	——
No extra words	——	——	——	——	——
Dialogue	——	——	——	——	——
Tone and rhythm	——	——	——	——	——

Composition skills

Plurals	——	——	——	——	——
Adjectives and adverbs	——	——	——	——	——
Proper verb use	——	——	——	——	——
Possessives	——	——	——	——	——
Word usage	——	——	——	——	——
Spelling	——	——	——	——	——
Punctuation	——	——	——	——	——

Writing Skills Inventory (continued)

	Weak	Fair	Strong	Don't Know	Not Relevant
Evaluating and rewriting skills	——	——	——	——	——
Skills for removing sexism from writing	——	——	——	——	——
Skills for writing for educational assignments					
Term papers	——	——	——	——	——
Laboratory reports	——	——	——	——	——
Book reports	——	——	——	——	——
Essay examinations	——	——	——	——	——
Theses and dissertations	——	——	——	——	——
Skills for writing for professional requirements					
Memos	——	——	——	——	——
Newsletters	——	——	——	——	——
Reports	——	——	——	——	——
Proposals	——	——	——	——	——

	Weak	Fair	Strong	Don't Know	Not Relevant
Skills for writing for publication					
Popular articles	____	____	____	____	____
Professional articles	____	____	____	____	____
Scholarly articles	____	____	____	____	____
Trade books	____	____	____	____	____
Professional books	____	____	____	____	____
Textbooks	____	____	____	____	____
Other writing skills	____	____	____	____	____

Your job requires—

_____

_____

_____

_____

_____

Writing Skills Learning Plan

What I Want to Learn   **By What Date**

1. _____   _____

_____

2. _____   _____

_____

3. _____   _____

_____

4. _____   _____

_____

How I Plan to Learn (attending a course, a reading program, etc.)

_____

_____

_____

_____

_____

When I Plan to Learn (my schedule)

_____

_____

_____

_____

What Constraints I Will Face   **How Resolved**

_____   _____

_____   _____

_____   _____

_____   _____

_____   _____

_____   _____

_____   _____

What I Learned

_____

_____

_____

_____

_____

_____

_____

_____

_____

Weekly Time Inventory

	Sunday	Monday	Tuesday	Wednesday	Thursday	Friday	Saturday
6:00 A.M.							
7:00							
8:00							
9:00							
10:00							
11:00							
12:00							
1:00 P.M.							
2:00							

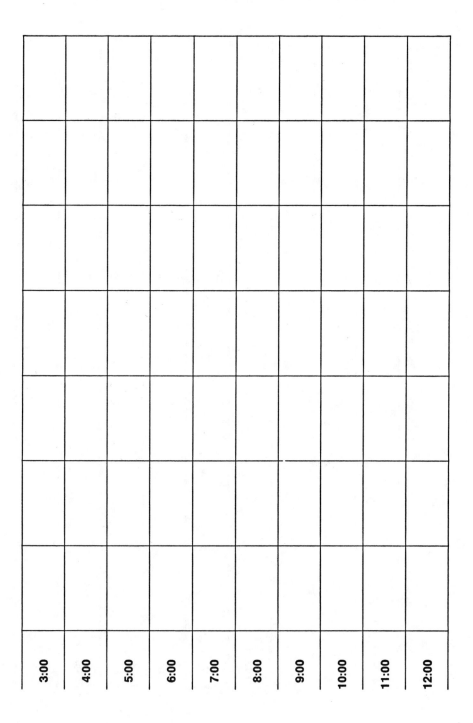

3:00

4:00

5:00

6:00

7:00

8:00

9:00

10:00

11:00

12:00

Weekly Time Plan

	Sunday	Monday	Tuesday	Wednesday	Thursday	Friday	Saturday
6:00 A.M.							
7:00							
8:00							
9:00							
10:00							
11:00							
12:00							
1:00 P.M.							
2:00							

3:00	4:00	5:00	6:00	7:00	8:00	9:00	10:00	11:00	12:00

Sample Permissions Request

Permissions Request

Date:

To:

I hereby request permission to reprint the material
described below:

Title of selection or description
of excerpt

_____

_____

_____

Page reference(s) _____

_____

Author of selection _____

Book or periodical title _____

_____

Author of book or periodical _____

_____

Copyright of book or periodical _____

I seek world rights for this selection in the book shown below and reprints and minor revisions thereof, including the right to license braille and large-type editions for the handicapped.

Title _____

_____

Author(s) _____

_____

Publisher _____

Approx. no. of pages _____ Binding _____

Probable publication date _____ Proposed net price _____

Size of printing _____

Market _____

Please specify below the credit line you require. A copy of this letter is enclosed for your files.

We hereby give permission for rights as indicated in the use of the above-mentioned material.

Permission authorized by

_____

Date _____

Commonly
Misspelled Words

Commonly Misspelled Words

accommodate	dessert	interrupt
accustomed	disastrous	lightning
analysis	dissatisfied	livelihood
analyze	embarrass	loneliness
appropriate	environment	loose
believe	equipped	lose
benefited	exhausted	miniature
business	existence	minimum
changeable	experience	misspelled
cloth	familiar	movable
clothes	fascinate	neither
compliment	forth	ninety
conquer	forty	noticeable
conscience	fourth	occasion
conscientious	government	occasionally
courteous	grammar	occur
criticism	guarantee	occurred
curriculum	hoping	occurrence
decision	hopping	parallel
desert	humorous	particularly
desirable	hurrying	permanent
desperate	incidentally	persistent

personally	separate	they're
piece	similar	though
preferred	speech	through
privilege	studying	transferred
quiet	succeed	truly
receive	success	twelfth
recommend	their	weather
referred	there	whether

Preparing Footnotes and Bibliographies

Preparing Footnotes

Two kinds of footnotes are commonly used: those that further explain something mentioned in the body of the text and those that refer to a source.

If the flow of your writing would be broken by adding explanatory material in the text, the explanatory footnote may be properly used. Excessively long explanatory footnotes should be avoided, however. The form of an explanatory footnote is to use declarative sentences in a simple conversational style. The tone of the explanatory footnote is along this line: "By the way, reader, here is something else about this that you may find interesting and useful to your understanding."

For reference footnotes, the style depends on the source. For reference to a book, a standard footnote lists the following: author's full name, complete title of the book (underlined), edition (if other than the first), place where published, publisher, date of publication, and page number(s) referred to. For example:

1. Mortimer J. Adler, Aristotle for Everybody: Difficult Thought Made Easy (New York: Macmillan, 1978), pp. 7–9.

For reference to an article in a periodical, the footnote should list the following: author's full name, title of article (in quotation marks), name of periodical (underlined), volume number of the periodical, date of the issue, and page number(s) referred to. For example:

1. P. A. Moenster, "Learning and Memory in Relation to Age," Journal of Gerontology 27 (1972): 361–363.

For more popular periodicals, the volume information is sometimes omitted. For example:

1. P. B. Baltes and K. W. Schaie, "The Myth of the Twilight Years," Psychology Today, March 1974, pp. 35–40.

When checking footnotes for accuracy, make certain that the author's name, title, and publisher's name are spelled correctly. Check to make certain that the punctuation for footnoting is consistent throughout your piece and the page numbers cited are accurate.

To indicate a footnote in a manuscript, type a raised number immediately following the word, phrase, or sentence in the text to which the footnote refers. For example:

His latest book, See Mary Fail,[1] has been widely reviewed.

The numbering of footnotes may (1) run consecutively throughout the piece, particularly if it is a shorter piece of writing, (2) begin again with each new page, or (3) begin again with each new chapter, especially in a longer work.

When placing footnotes at the bottom of the page, type a solid line of approximately twenty strokes to separate the footnotes from the copy above. Type the solid line two spaces below the last line, beginning at the left side of the page. Double-space and then begin typing the footnotes. Begin each footnote with its number typed on the line and followed by a period. (Note: When typing material for publication, type all footnotes double spaced on a separate sheet of paper.)

Preparing a Bibliography

The bibliography appears at the end of your work. The style of a bibliographic entry depends on the reference.

For a book entry: name of author(s), editor(s), or agency or institution responsible for writing the material when no author is mentioned; complete title of the book, including the subtitle if there is one; edition (if not the original); place of publication; publisher's name; date of publication. For example:

Bolles, Richard Nelson. The Three Boxes of Life. Berkeley, Calif.: Ten Speed Press, 1978.

For an article in a periodical: name of author(s), title of article, name of periodical, volume number or date or both. For example:

Ohliger, John. "Radical Ideas in Adult Education: A Manifesto-Bibliography." Radical Teacher, May 1979.

An excellent source for detailed information about footnotes, bibliographies, and a host of other matters related to writing style is the thirteenth edition of the University of Chicago Press's *Chicago Manual of Style*. A condensed paperback version is Kate Turabian's *Manual for Writers of Term Papers, Theses, and Dissertations* (Chicago: University of Chicago Press, 1973).

Sample Newsletters

CREDIT UNION Leadership Letter

WEEKLY NEWSLETTER OF THE CREDIT UNION NATIONAL ASSOCIATION, INC. / BOX 431 / MADISON. WIS. 53701

April 20, 1981

N.C. SUPREME COURT STRIKES DOWN CU BYLAW   The North Carolina supreme court has struck down a bylaw amendment that would have opened membership in State ECU, Raleigh, N.C., to an estimated 55,000 new potential members.

The bylaw would have allowed the CU to serve employees of governmental units covered by the state retirement system, employees of agencies subject to the state personnel act, and federal employees working with those units, plus retirees and family members.

The amendment was approved by the state CU commission in 1978, but was challenged in court by banking and S&L interests. After a series of appeals it reached the supreme court last year.

The supreme court held in its 5-2 decision that the CU commission had misinterpreted the state CU act in approving the bylaw amendment, and sent the case back to Wake County Superior Court, where the case originated, for entry of a final judgment and disposition.

Bobby Hall, vice-president of State ECU, said last week that in the nine-month period following the CU commission's approval of the bylaw, State ECU had taken in nearly 9,000 new members under the amended field of membership. These members, he said, have about $1 million in shares and $1 million in loans outstanding.

The CU is now concerned, he said, with what the lower court will require the CU to do with those members. He said the CU hoped the court would allow them to maintain their savings through the current dividend period and to pay off their loans according to contract.

Curtis Ring, vice-president of the North Carolina League, said the league will be working with State ECU and the supervisory agency to try to maintain CU services for these members.

Hall said he expected the Wake County court to enter its final judgment within two to three weeks.

CD OFFERS SHOULD CALL FOR CAUTION   CUs receiving telephone calls from brokers who offer certificates of deposit at 10 to 50 basis points above market rates "should immediately raise a red flag of caution," U.S. Central CU general manager Jim Kudlinski said this week in a "warning to investors."

Kudlinski said that a number of CUs have reportedly received such calls from brokers recently, and added that the incidence is likely to increase.

The offers, Kudlinski said, usually involve jumbo CDs from S&Ls at rates 10 to 50 or more basis points above current market rates.

"When they're offering CDs at above-market rates," Kudlinski said, "it has to be for a reason. And the reason is probably that the soundness of the issuing institution is questionable."

He cautioned CU managers and investment officers against "chasing off after high yields" without investigating the offer thoroughly.

"An investigation is even more important," he said, "if it's a broker you've never dealt with, or an institution you've never heard of."

Kudlinski recommended contacting the CU's corporate central for information and guidance.

TAX PAYMENTS THROW CURVE AT $ SUPPLY   Observers of the money supply will probably be more confused than ever this week--one in which the money supply typically fluctuates wildly due to the April 15 tax deadline.

Both tax payments and the speed of processing refund checks affect the money supply data--but this year some taxpayers are expected to pay taxes with drafts drawn on money market funds. The funds have no direct impact on the money supply, but they are expected to add even more uncertainty to the figures.

April 20, 1981   LEADERSHIP LETTER   Page Four

LIQUIDATIONS OF FCUs PEAKED IN 1980: NCUA   A record 326 FCUs entered liquidation in 1980, according to figures released recently by NCUA, but officials have indicated that the situation is probably improving.

Difficult economic conditions, competition from money market mutual funds, and unrealistically low loan interest ceilings during 1980 were among the reasons cited by NCUA for the record number of liquidations.

NCUA said the number of FCUs liquidated in 1980 was 18% greater than the previous record of 277 recorded in 1979. The number of involuntary liquidations--258--was nearly 53% above the previous high of 169 in 1979, NCUA said.

The 68 voluntary liquidations recorded by FCUs in 1980 represented a decrease from the 108 voluntary liquidations in 1979, NCUA said.

Of the 258 FCUs placed in involuntary liquidation last year, NCUA said, plant closings were a factor in 56 closings. Delinquent loans were a problem with about half the FCUs forced to close, NCUA indicated. Other problems leading to liquidation, NCUA said, included compliance problems, lax or deficient elected leadership, ineffective management, and record-keeping deficiencies.

Although NCUA did not give the typical size of liquidating FCUs, most were believed to be small.

DoD ISSUES POLICY ON CU UTILITIES   The Department of Defense has issued a directive ordering military commands to furnish janitorial services, utilities, fixtures and maintenance at no cost to defense CUs at one location--a policy change long sought by the Defense CU Council.

The directive is effective April 1 as a policy, although each service must issue an implementing directive before local commanders can carry it out, the Defense Council said. The Defense Department gives the services 120 days to implement directives, DCUC said.

The change had been sought by the Defense Council after Navy FCU conducted a study and submitted it to the Navy Department in 1979. The campaign was led by Vice Adm. Vincent Lascara, president of Navy FCU and a DCUC director.

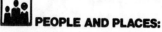

PEOPLE AND PLACES:

LAURES NAMED IOWA LEAGUE CHAIRMAN   Raymond J. Laures, president of Oscar Mayer ECU, Davenport, has been re-elected chairman of the Iowa League. The action came last week at the league's 1981 annual meeting.

Past CUNA Vice-Chairman Lee E. Tucker has stepped down after 17 years as general manager of D-M FCU, Phoenix, Ariz., citing medical reasons. Glen E. Hendrix succeeds him.

Robert Schaffner, past president of the Defense CU Council, will retire next month after 23 years as manager of Fort Knox FCU, Kentucky.

James McCormack, senior planning consultant for CMCI Corp., has been named vice-president, finance and administration, for the Pennsylvania League. The appointment becomes effective May 11.

The Iowa League is seeking applications for the position of president, a post that becomes vacant Dec. 31 when A. W. Jordan retires. Resumes should be sent to Raymond J. Laures, chairman of the screening committee, care of Oscar Mayer ECU, 1400 Rockingham Rd., Davenport, Iowa 52802, to arrive by June 30.

Donald Beall, Robert Byroad, Paul Dickerson and Mike Flaherty have been re-elected directors of Capital Corporate FCU. Beall is president of the FCU.

Wylma Tilton, Collins ECU, Cedar Rapids, has been named to the Iowa Commerce Commission's consumer council.

The North Dakota League has a new street address: 2005 N. Kavaney Drive, Bismarck, N.D. The mailing address remains Box 1956, Bismarck, N.D. 58501.

IOWA LEAGUE NOW HAS ONE NON-AFFILIATE   Only one of Iowa's 368 CUs remains unaffiliated with the Iowa League, following the affiliation last week of Des Moines Police Officers CU for the first time ever.

The affiliation was approved by the delegates at the league's recent annual meeting.

Des Moines Police Officers CU has 457 members and at year-end 1980 had assets of $1,996,561. Police Chief Billie B. Wallace is president of the CU.

RITUALS OF THE EARTH

A Newsletter of the Sigurd Olson Environmental Institute   •   Northland College   •   Ashland, WI
VOL. 2, NO. 2   SPRING 1981

Special Issue: Children & The Environment

Can You Teach a Sense of Wonder?

The Environmental Learning Center at Isabella would like to try. With the help of the Sigurd Olson Environmental Institute at Northland College in Ashland, Wisconsin, perhaps it can.

"For a long time I have felt that there was something missing from our curriculum," said ELC Director Jack Pichotta. "We have great natural history classes and superb teachers. The combination of the two instills a sense of curiosity, of respect for living things in most kids. But it seems that should happen by design, not just by chance."

The impetus for Jack's enthusiasm for this curriculum change came largely from a seminar he attended in 1980 that was sponsored by the Institute. Some 40 other camp directors, business people, Native Americans and church people gathered in Madison, Wisconsin, to explore the spiritual roots of how to care for the earth in the '80s. It was an opportunity for all those individuals concerned about the stewardship of the earth's resources to discuss, share and unite.

"It (the conference) made me feel like a born again earthling," said Jack. His comment elicited chuckles of agreement from members of the Institute who were present to launch a plan of followup action to the conference.

"It seems like all of us became interested in environmental education and environmental issues for that same, almost intangible reason," agreed Rev. Phillip Garrison, St. John's Church, LaPointe, Wis. "It's important to bring that feeling of excitement and commitment to the forefront."

"It seems like we're almost apologetic for those feelings of dedication," said Marina Herman, of the Institute staff. "It's gotten so we're trained to keep those spiritual feelings out of our conversations, especially when we're dealing with the business/political world. And that's not healthy."

A Plan for Action

As a result of a February 9 meeting at the Institute, the following agreement between the ELC and the Institute has been worked out:

1) Four adult workships will be held at the ELC during the 1981-1982 school year. The workshops will be open to teachers, parents and other persons interested in exploring the spiritual and philosophical foundations of the environmental movement. They will be conducted by the Institute and will attempt to:

a. Increase the sensitivity of each person attending to his own stewardship with the earth's resources.

b. Help devise action plans for conference attendees so they can share that sensitivity with their students or children.

2) Several new program units will be written for the ELC which deal specifically with the topic of stewardship of the earth.

3) A May planning meeting will be held between Institute personnel, ELC staff and other interested persons to get more input on number 1) and 2) and to launch other program ideas on this topic. Anyone with ideas or with an interest in attending is encouraged to contact ELC Director Jack Pichotta or Marina Herman from the Institute.

The ELC will benefit from the expertise of the Institute. The Institute will benefit by having a host for its workshops. Both are excited about working together in this vital area of environmental education.

by Ann Schimpf,
OPENINGS Editor
Environmental Learning Center

Everything new and pure
in the very prime of the spring
when Nature's pulses were beating
highest and mysteriously
keeping time with our own!
Young hearts, young leaves,
flowers, animals,
the winds and the streams
and the sparkling lake, all wildly,
gladly rejoicing together!

John Muir

Page 2

STAFF PERSPECTIVES

A column written by a staff member of the Religion & Environment Project.

Jack Pichotta,
Executive Director
Environmental Learning Center

When I was a sixth grader attending Irving Elementary School in West Duluth I know for certain that I didn't know what an environmentalist was and that I probably never used the term environment. I've a hunch that my mother and dad, and even my school teachers didn't have much use for the words either. Looking from my office window today, on an unseasonally wet and windy April 1st, thirty-three years later, I see small groups of sixth grade scholars learning about the environment. Words like "habitat", "pH" and "succession" find logical use in their discussion. Desks and tablets have been replaced by wet-weather gear and clipboards. Books, while important in the classroom setting, have been replaced by such things as task-cards, binoculars, bottom dredges and kits for measuring dissolved oxygen. An ever increasing number of today's young children know about the environment.

Earth Day launched what will certainly come to be recognized as the Decade of the Environment. Individuals and groups of individuals concerned about air and water quality, as well as aspects of land use, joined forces and discovered that the democratic system really works. Major changes were legislated, and, as should have been expected, reaction to the changes grew. By the end of the decade, everyone knew and used the word environmentalist, but the emphasis had changed.

Environmental education grew during the seventies too. New courses and activities sprang up almost overnight in the nation's elementary and secondary schools. Colleges and universities introduced courses and even rewarded degrees in the field of environmental education. In Minnesota the number of resident facilities available for school environmental education trips grew from just a few to over fifty.

While a great deal of valuable environmental education takes place in the traditional classroom setting, an ever increasing amount of this learning is happening where people live, work and play. The definition of teacher is changing too. Classroom teachers have found eager helpers from the ranks of parents and community leaders. At the resident facilities, a new breed of teacher/interpreter has evolved and
continued on page seven

RITUALS OF THE EARTH is a special newsletter published by the Sigurd Olson Environmental Institute of Northland College in Ashland, Wisconsin.

The Institute coordinates a broad range of educational programs such as workshops, seminars, lectures and community involvement efforts aimed at enhancing life in the northern region. Since 1972, the Institute, guided by the philosophy of Sigurd F. Olson, has disseminated information on environmental and natural resource concerns of the Lake Superior region.

SIGURD OLSON
ENVIRONMENTAL INSTITUTE
Northland College
Ashland, Wisconsin 54806
(715) 682-4531, ext. 223

Tom Klein, *Director*
Harriet Irwin, *Education Director*
Steve Sorensen, *Community Specialist*
Arnell Lavasseur   Don Albrecht   Bill Otis
    Secretary   *Horizons Editor Voyageur Director*
Glen Nagel, *EE Coordinator;* Sue Ellen Smith, *AV Coordinator;* Jim Pierce, *Project Loon Watch;* Kim Laru, *Librarian*
Special Projects: Marina Herman, Lisa Kennedy, Dick Rice, Laurie Rogers, Cathy Caliendo.
Artwork by: Jamila Larson (age 7), Mark Garrison (age 11), Jennifer Garrison (age 12).

EDITOR'S CORNER

55° in the middle of March! I found myself hurrying to lace up my boots, put my son Benjamin in the backpack and dash out the front door to discover what else was awakening from its Winter's sleep.

Over the hill, past the planted flower beds where tulips were now 4 inches high, daffodils, iris, hyacinths and crocus were pushing through the warmed soil. Ben and I walked past the melting snowdrifts, bidding it a joyous farewell. The dogs ran in front of us—treading lightly on the pond's thin ice, skirting just around the edges. We all dashed into the woods to smell the sap, see the buds swelling on the poplar—even looking for signs of asparagus, though we knew it wouldn't be up for another month. But we were so excited to hear so many birds calling, to see green!

I remembered so many of those earlier Spring days when my two sisters, my brother and I would venture out into our backyard swamp to discover so many of the same things. I couldn't help dreaming of the time when my husband and I would walk with Benjamin through the woods and rediscover with him all the excitement and energy of Spring.

This issue of RITUALS hopes to capture some of that same excitement and energy and share it with you. It is dedicated to the same sense of wonder we see in Spring and in children. It seeks to give you ideas, tools and resources to rediscover the earth and celebrate the gift of a child's enthusiasm and wonder. MERRY SPRING!

Marina Lachecki Herman

Guidelines for Preparing Manuscripts

All material intended for publication—including footnotes, bibliographies, and quotations—should be typed double spaced. Use 20-pound rag bond paper. If you are submitting an article for publication, use the following format when typing the first page of your manuscript:

Your name   Approximate number of words
Address, phone number

Title of Article
by
Your Name

Type your name in the upper left-hand corner of all succeeding pages of the manuscript. Send the manuscript flat in a large envelope and include a self-addressed, stamped envelope in case it is rejected.

Increasingly, writers are using word processors in place of typewriters. A word processor combines a typewriter keyboard with a television screen and a microcomputer and allows you to revise and re-write your material before it's even on paper. Words can be removed or added with the stroke of a key; paragraphs and entire sections can be moved around. Programs are available that will go through your writing and spot words for consistency and spelling. Writers who use word processors say their efficiency has increased manyfold.

Although your manuscript should be as clean as possible, it need not be retyped whenever you wish to revise something. For those who do not have access to word processors, here are some tech-niques commonly used during the process of revising a manuscript.

If you wish to insert a word or phrase in a sentence, indicate by marking a caret ($\wedge$) where the insertion is to be made. Then write the insertion above the line, never below it.

If you wish to add an entire paragraph or more to the manuscript, draw a caret and a line from the place where you wish to add the material to the margin and write, "Insert A" (or whatever the materi-al's designation might be). For example:

Sometimes writing can be exceedingly tedious, $\wedge$ but writing skills are necessary for a person who wishes to get ahead.

Type the added material on a separate sheet marked, "Insert A," and insert it following the page in the manuscript where it is to appear. When a paragraph is out of place, circle it and give it a letter designa-tion too (for example, Insert B). Then write, "Insert B," where you believe the paragraph fits better.

If you're adding entire pages to the manuscript, indicate where the additional pages are to go and then number them a, b, c, etc., begin-ning with the page number where the addition begins. For instance, if the added material is to begin on page 16, the additional pages would be numbered 16a, 16b, and so on.

If you need to add many pages, move around several paragraphs, or make many inserts, it's best to retype the material. Otherwise, your reviewer will become hopelessly interrupted by constantly turn-ing back and forth in your manuscript to the point where the flow of the reading is lost.

When marking a final revision for typing, you should know and use some common proofreader's marks. They are shortcuts and save time. If your material is accepted for publication, editors expect you to use proofreader's marks when making corrections on proofs. Fol-lowing are some common proofreader's marks.

Mark	Explanation	Example in Copy
⊙	Put in period	The end ⊙
⌄	Put in apostrophe	Joe⌄s machine
⌄	Put in comma	"Yes⌄" he said.
⌄⌄	Put in quotation marks	⌄Yes,⌄ he said.
? (set)	Put in question mark	"Now ? " she asked.
⌐	Move left	⌐It's time.
⌐	Move right	⌐Read carefully.
¶	Start paragraph	It's over. ⌐ Sometimes
No ¶	No paragraph	ran quickly. Furthermore
(sp)	Spell it out	(U.S.) Congress
caps	Use capital letters	joe smith
lc	Use lowercase letters	White Oak
ital	Set in italic type	a rich person
◡	Close up completely	writ ing well
◡	Take it out	too much much tea
stet	Let it stay	a careless writer
#	Put in space	whiteoak

Index